JUGGLING
DYNAMITE

JUGGLING
DYNAMITE

An insider's wisdom about money
management, markets, and wealth that lasts

Danielle Park

INSOMNIAC PRESS

Library and Archives Canada Cataloguing in Publication

Park, Danielle, 1965-   Juggling dynamite : an insider's wisdom about money management, markets, and wealth that lasts / Danielle Park.

Includes index. ISBN 978-1-897178-34-8

1. Finance, Personal. 2. Investments. I. Title.
HG179.P39 2007   332.024'01   C2007-901107-1

The publisher gratefully acknowledges the support of the Department of Canadian Heritage through the Book Publishing Industry Development Program.

Printed and bound in Canada

Insomniac Press, 192 Spadina Avenue, Suite 403
Toronto, Ontario, Canada, M5T 2C2
www.insomniacpress.com

Canadä

For Quinn and Spencer:
What we've learned so far...
Love Mom

Acknowledgements

This book had been in my plans for a long time. I am glad to have it finally out of my head. Acknowledging all those who have helped me complete this task could be lengthy; I will be succinct.

This book captures a lifetime of mentors and inverse mentors who have brought me a rich breadth of experience. First, I wish to acknowledge Irene, Gilbert, and Mary, three of the best grandparents a kid could ever have the privilege of growing up around. Their gifts of wisdom, experience, and time generously invested in me are forever helpful. I am also indebted to my parents, Tom and Norinne, for their example of non-conventional thinking and passionate living that conditioned me from an early age to measure success more in quality of life than quantity of goods.

I am indebted to some truly great teachers in my life who encouraged and inspired me to write and think critically from an early age, most notably my mom, Beverly Rumble, and Rosemary Sullivan.

Thank you to my assistant Colleen for her excellent support over the past many years, which has helped me to carve out time for writing and teaching on top of a busy practice. Thank you to Ann for her five years as our loving nanny who helped us raise a young family and continue a career.

I am grateful for my publisher, Mike O'Connor, at Insomniac Press for taking a leap of faith with me. And to my editor,

Dan Varrette, for his diligent and patient work in knocking my rambling thoughts into shape on the page.

I am very thankful for the time and feedback of a few key people who have encouraged me to complete this book and who served as the first trusted eyes to review early drafts. In particular, Lisa Walters, Howard Gwin, Isabelle Gagnon, and George Taylor. I will always remember your kind support.

In my own education about money, I am humbly indebted to some sage voices who have gone before me: John Kenneth Galbraith, Peter L. Bernstein, Benjamin Graham, Warren Buffett, and John Templeton, to name a few. I offer these mentors much credit for that which may be worthy in this book. Any errors or misstatements are mine alone. I am also indebted to many clients, colleagues, and students over the years who have helped me learn important lessons about all of us.

Finally, I am indebted to my partner in life and in work, Cory Venable, a gifted market analyst and fiercely independent thinker who has been my constant sounding board through the failures, revelations, and triumphs of the past twenty years. Our joint evolution has been so collaborative it is in many ways our collective thoughts and experience that form this book. Your faithful friendship remains my greatest reward.

Table of Contents

Preface

As a money manager, I am focused first on protecting capital from blowing up. Investing requires a lot of measuring and estimating, a process highly charged with the emotions of the investment creators, marketers, and holders. For this reason, investments can be like lit dynamite: remarkably volatile and full of risk. Once destroyed, invested capital and precious time are lost forever. In this sense, a money manager's role can be likened to that of a professional dynamite juggler. Many investors cannot see the risks involved until a pick ends badly. Many do not even realize the fuses are lit until an explosion goes off, and when it does, most are surprised by the extent of the damage caused.

It was an interest in connecting key themes noted throughout my professional career over the past twenty years that brought this collection of thoughts to paper. This is not a financial planning book or a finance text. The purpose is to highlight some of the pitfalls in our human behaviour around money so that we may see truth and gain insight, waste less and benefit more. Furthermore, it is my purpose to confront the self-serving rhetoric of investment sales and demonstrate why objective discipline and market cycle timing are critical to lasting success for real-life investors.

We live in a time when we have access to more information than ever before, and yet its true utility often remains unclear. People today are perhaps more informed but generally, it seems, not very enlightened. It is my hope that this book will be useful to readers seeking clarity.

I have included a bibliography of key books that I believe all investors should read. I have compiled this list as I have discovered them one by one over the years. With much sales puff in the field of investing, finding the truly useful books can be challenging and yet critical, in my view, to lasting success.

Section I

The Fuse:
People and Their Markets

Chapter 1
The Truth about Human Nature

It is human nature to think wisely and act foolishly.
—Anatole France

Many of us are not ready to hear the truth. We would rather continue living in a bubble. But if the bubble were to burst, our worldview would be forever altered. As in all things, our understanding of money must start at the beginning. Although some people do win the lottery, for most of us, the key to lasting financial success is constant, conservative, diligent discipline and self-restraint. And if this last point doesn't cause you to close this book and toss it in the bin, there is hope. You can learn this stuff, and you don't need a graduate degree in finance to be wise about money.

Throughout my life, I have noticed that people generally fall into one of two camps. One is the "I know nothing about money" camp. These people believe that finance and investing are very complicated and that they know nothing about them. This is partly what the financial industry likes us to believe, because it serves their purpose in two ways: first, if it is all very complicated, then we need "an expert" to show us the way. Second, if everything is so complicated, then we are less able to follow the pea under the shell as it is shuffled around in front of our eyes. Believing we know nothing about money and investing is actually a dangerous cop out. If we are going to have some money and live in our modern world, we need to stop throwing our hands up and start doing some real work listening, reading, and learning. A fool and his money are soon parted, so we need to get a grip—and the sooner, the better.

As a money manager, when clients tell me they understand nothing about money, up raises a red flag of caution. They often say that they don't need to understand since they have hired me to do it for them. This tends to cause everyone great unhappiness. First, if a person has no understanding, then they also will lack the self-discipline that flows from understanding. A client must be aware of the dangers to know why their leader is taking them around a longer route. If not, they may follow for a short while, but ultimately they will grow impatient and begin to complain that their leader is wasting their time. Clients can be attracted to those who offer them shortcuts, not realizing that they must blindly wade through landmines along those routes. At the peak of each financial bubble, it happens repeatedly that the wisest, most prudent managers are fired for being too conservative and risk-averse. Victims don't often see the importance of alarm bells and a breaker system until after disaster has struck.

Over the years, I have met people who have explained they don't need to know about money because they can rely on their parents, spouse, or partner who have it all worked out. Others will explain that they don't need to know about money because they are rich and money is not a worry. These are famous last words! If we rely on friends and family to look after all our money decisions, we may be placing ourselves in peril. People die, spouses leave, and fortunes are lost. No one should be without good knowledge and skill in financial matters. Financial ignorance can be very expensive. Consider how many of the *Forbes* richest people in the world fall off the annual list within twenty years. The answer is 87%.

The second camp, of which there are fewer but still significant numbers, is the "I am very smart and educated about other things and so I am sophisticated and naturally know a lot about investing." This group tends to be very hazardous to its own financial health and sometimes to the financial health of others around it. These people have generally had some success either in another profession or in business. They are undoubtedly experts in their own area, but they make the catastrophic assumption that being able to make money in business makes one brilliant in general. "Financial genius is before the fall," economist John Kenneth Galbraith warns us in his book *A Short History of Financial Euphoria*. The ancient Greek term for this is *hubris*: the tragic flaw of the heroes who fall in love with their own intelligence or ideas.

In our financial affairs, it is important to our success that we face the facts. The first thing someone looking for "the truth" should do is read Galbraith's book. It's a quick read, but it's an excellent starting place in the journey to financial enlightenment. Beware, however: Galbraith does not pull any punches. He ominously warns us about one of our greatest human flaws: our "specious association of money and intelligence":

> In all free-enterprise (once called capitalist) attitudes there is a strong tendency to believe that the more money, either as income or assets, of which an individual is possessed or with which he is associated, the deeper and more compelling his economic and social perception, the more astute and penetrating his mental processes ... this is readily transmuted by

the recipient into an assurance of personal mental superiority. Treated that way, I must be wise. In consequence, self-scrutiny—the greatest support to minimal good sense—is at risk.[1]

We should print off these words and post them somewhere so that we can see them every day as we journey through life. The daily discipline of keeping our ego in check is a key to long-lasting success. As a famous economist, Galbraith spent a prolific career in counsel with political and business leaders and scholars. And yet, throughout, he maintained the pragmatic core of the Ontario farm boy he had been. He saw that a material society too easily equates assets and income with wisdom and intelligence, often granting credit where little or none is due.

There are many reasons why people seem to have money and these may be quite unrelated to their intelligence or personal acumen. Money can be won, inherited, and even stolen. The point is that we are foolish if we assume that just because someone has it, or appears to have it, they must be smart, good, or worthy of trust.

I recall my first glimpses of these notions when I was a young lawyer working as a junior on a number of high-society divorce files. At the time, I was earning $23,000 a year and was up to my neck in student loans. One of our clients owned a number of walk-in dental clinics and was obviously loaded. He drove a fleet of exotic cars, wore designer clothing, lived in what seemed to me a palace, and generally had the "I am very smart and successful" air to go with it all. I was certainly quite impressed, I can tell you. It was my job to have him prepare financial statements for the court proceeding. He gave me his very impressive income figures—he made $1 million a year (a daunting figure to me then). He had a long list of boats and cars and every possible toy, and he had a negative net worth! I could not believe my eyes when I calculated the columns on his debts versus assets. How could this guy who had been making a million bucks a year for a few years have had a negative net worth? My mind was boggled.

What many people don't get is that making money is quite different from *having* money, and having money is not necessarily a static condition—it means that you must *keep* it once obtained. Keeping it means you have to be careful, frugal, and generally respectful of your money. The concentrated risks that one may take to make money in the first place, either through occupation or business, are quite often the things one must avoid exposing that money to again if it is to be protected and endure. No matter how wealthy we may be, we can never afford to become cocky or blasé. Witness Conrad Black in the news of late. Lord Black is one of the wealthiest guys in Canada (or at least used to be). Incredible fortunes have a nasty habit of reversing once common sense, humility, and self-scrutiny are lost.

People who are easily distracted from the donut often end up with only the hole. To give wealth and income earned some context, consider this: in order for a forty-year-old to collect an after-tax income of $1 million a year for the rest of their life, they would need to have in excess of $50 million carefully and conservatively invested.[2] Less than 85,000 people in the world have that much money. Less than nine million people in the world have more than a million dollars outside of their own home and contents. That is less than 0.14% of the world population, or just 1,300 people in a million worldwide.[3] And yet, besieged by the marketing machine of popular culture, many in our society believe that most people have more money than they actually do.

World Wealth in Perspective

	Population	% of World Population*
High Net Worth Individuals (Those with net financial assets greater than US$1 million)	8.7 million	0.137
Ultra-High Net Worth Individuals (Those with net financial assets greater than US$30 million)	85,400	0.00137
Billionaires	793	0.000012

World population 6,551,205,725
Source: World Wealth Report 2006, www.capgemini.com

We compare our lifestyle to the pictures in celebrity and fashion magazines and deem that we fall far short. We feel like underachievers in comparison to the wealth we perceive in others. Once we see the world this way, we think there must be some trick or shortcut to getting into a more elite club. Whether we acknowledge it or not, many of us make the pursuit of this perceived wealth the main focus of living. There is always hope for the great easy: a way to get rich without real work. This is the underlying promise of the marketing machine that surrounds investment sales. It is the real reason otherwise sane people agree to hold dynamite in the first place.

Properly invested to preserve the capital, $1 million will produce a maximum pre-tax income of about $50,000 per year. In this sense, people earning annual salaries of $50,000 are already living on an income as though they were millionaires. Few of them would think of their financial status in such favourable terms. When people have the good fortune of winning or inheriting $1 million, it is often blown quickly, as recipients erroneously believe such a stipend can afford them lavish things. Ignorance and unreasonable expectations around money are a common plight.

So the first thing we have to do is get realistic and stop thinking apparent wealth is true wealth, or that earning a big income solves all the problems, or that people who seem to have money must also have all the answers. There is a lot more to this.

The most constant impediment to our financial success is human nature. We are impulsive animals by origin and nature. We can be enormously influenced by emotional swings and faulty logic. It is difficult to maintain an objective self-view, and this is especially true when it comes to our money. We hope for many things, but we must be very careful that our hope is not the only thing driving our money decisions. We may hope to win the lottery or strike it rich overnight, but we must plan our actions for the likelihood of these things not being our fate. Harvard Ph.D. Terry Burnham calls the impulsive side of our decision-making our "lizard brain." He points out that the animal skills that evolved to help us forage for food and find shelter tend to be exactly out of synch with financial opportunity.

…our brains, like our bodies, reflect the world of our ancestors. In particular, our lizard brains are pattern-seeking, backward-looking systems that allowed us to forage for food, and repeat successful behaviours. This system helped our ancestors survive and repro-duce, but financial markets punish such backward-looking decisions. Consequently, our lizard brains tend to make us buy at market tops and sell at market bottoms.[4]

We have a tendency to be aggressive when we should be careful and afraid when we should be confident. In money matters, these traits become the mirror peaks of fear and greed that continually threaten sound financial decisions.

Another theory that informs this area of human behaviour is something called "EQ," or "emotional quotient." Psychologists John D. Mayer and Peter Salovey wrote a series of papers on this topic in the early '90s, and Daniel Goleman further developed the concept in a 1995 book entitled *Emotional Intelligence.*

Their collective theory was developed out of combined research in neurophysiology, psychology, and cognitive science. In the end, they conclude that EQ, the ability to perceive and understand one's emotional responses, can be more important than IQ in determining how a person perceives and responds to the world. In the area of money and investing, I believe that their research is highly relevant.

I have noted this phenomenon many times over the years, where people who were undoubtedly intelligent and well educated repeatedly made poor decisions when it came to their money and investing. As a naive undergraduate student, I believed that the people with MBAs, CFAs, and Ph.D.s in finance were the best equipped to advise on investing. I have since seen how little academic learning can guarantee one's success with money. Many of my professors who held multiple degrees in finance and business often admitted that they had repeatedly suffered painful losses to their own capital. I have come to understand what economist and teacher Benjamin Graham meant when he wrote that successful investing is more a trait of the character than of the intellect. John Kenneth Galbraith said, "One of the greatest pieces of economic wisdom is to know what you do not know." So, humility is important, and the dangerous challenge to humility is hubris.

I once met with a fortysomething dot-com guy who had

been referred to our firm for investment counselling. He had cashed out his shares on an IPO at the peak of the tech market bubble in the late '90s and went from earning a good salary to having $50 million in the bank at one fell swoop. Unfortunately, dot-com guy didn't realize he had won the lottery. He seemed to believe that his newfound wealth was the natural product of his superior vision and intelligence. We call this "losing your nut" in my house. He took the hour of our interview to lecture me on why he was not in favour of diversification or bonds or capital preservation as a main focus of an investment policy. He was interested in high-risk investing and spoke of the "obvious" fact that high risk means high reward. I will make a prediction: the dot-com guy and his money have a high probability of being parted. It may take some time, and yes, he could win the lottery another couple of times, but the law of averages will prevail. There is a reason Las Vegas is very rich: high-risk rollers will eventually lose large amounts of money. Having $50 million deposited into a bank account does not mean that wisdom is deposited with it.

Wisdom is found through real-life experience and humility, and for many people, painful losses are required before the penny will drop. I have learned by observing human behaviour that the money-wise tend to be those who have suffered losses and have resolved to learn from past weaknesses. That said, there is still hope that if people can appreciate their own fallible nature in advance and set up guardrails to guide their path, great loss can be avoided or at least experienced with much less frequency.

There are a lot of harmful ideas about money that permeate our culture. There is the school of thought, widely held, that believes when you have lots of money, you can afford to waste it. "If you have to ask the price, you can't afford it." What utter rubbish. Some of the wisest wealthiest people I know are also the most careful with how they spend money. They know that money is a scarce commodity and that no matter how big your pile may be, it is, after all, a finite pile. If you spend or lose too much of it, it will disappear. And in a world where there is great need, wise people understand that money is a resource not to be squandered. Cost should always matter. Contrary to popular advertising, very few wealthy people actually hire private jets to tour the world on their own tab. It is much more common that such excesses are indulged in when a public corporation is paying for the extravagance.

It's easier to spend other people's money than it is to spend one's own. I will always remember the story of a former politician who used a fleet of jets to fly a fleet of black Mercedes cars to whichever country he was visiting. He did this to ensure that his entourage left the airport in a manner befitting his stature. The politician was not spending his own cash to support such a demonstration; the poor taxpayers were the unsuspecting patrons. Meanwhile, the rest of us who feel like paupers tend to marvel at such displays: "When you have that much money, you are in a different league, I guess!" No, when you spend money that frivolously, it is still a great waste. It does not make us common to ask the price of something to assess its value for its price.

While I was waitressing my way through university, I had the good fortune of serving many people from all walks of life. Much can be observed about human nature from the vantage point of a server. The owner of one of the restaurants I worked in was a self-made millionaire who had founded a chain of stores and later sold them to a larger chain. His new second wife at twentysomething was some thirty years his junior. Sadly, the millionaire had a massive heart attack one day and died in his office. The young widow spent the next few years embroiled in some nasty litigation with the millionaire's former wife and children. Word was that the estate topped many millions, so in the end, even after considerable litigation, the estate was divided and all were well-to-do.

The young widow then became famous in town as the prize catch, being both attractive and young in addition to being loaded. Unfortunately, wisdom was not as much in supply. A decade later, she had married a fast-talking man who acted with great confidence and importance in all of his affairs. He and the now thirtysomething wife were the toast of the town and invited to all of the most important social events. When others spoke of the couple, it was generally with awe as people clamoured to say that they had dined with them last week or golfed with them yesterday.

No one seemed to know quite what the husband did for money, but presuming that he had access to the wife's enormous stash, he naturally was invited to partner in various ventures with other local investors. The husband even set up his own business office with the outrageous title "financial advisor" posted on the door. With one failed venture after another, five years later, the fast-talker had fled town and the wife was left, now fortysomething, hiding from creditors she could not pay. The endless supply of money had been spent. In less than fifteen years, the famous "richest woman in town" was declaring personal bankruptcy.

Despite such stories being fairly common, the disastrous ending seems to take many by surprise. There is a seductive pull to the apparently rich. Simply the appearance of having money grants them certain fame. Too often, those around them see what they want to see and hear what they hope for. Many believe that wealth and good fortune may somehow rub off and that people with money can teach us the trick. People easily put themselves in harm's way, searching for the trick or the shortcut to wealth. This makes them highly susceptible to false messengers who pump the sunshine and tell us what we would like to hear. As an investment counsellor, I frequently meet people with low risk-tolerance looking for double-digit annual returns on their portfolios. When I tell them why they are expecting too much and should save more and spend less in order to grow their money, they are sceptical. They tell me that a financial planner or stockbroker has assured them that they can earn 12% per year and withdraw 10% per year in income throughout retirement. "Well, that's not a sustainable plan," I tell them. "It is all but certain to fail." At least half will thank me for my time and never darken my door again.

To put things into perspective, consider that given long-term investment returns in financial markets, $5 million in an investment account will produce an income net of tax of about $175,000 per year.[5] This amount of income may be considered comfortable for some, but is it rich? It is certainly not rich enough to live the lifestyles that upscale commercials and magazines urge us to pursue. The reality is that most people today who aspire to a life of material affluence are supporting their habits through escalating amounts of borrowed money. Spending money we don't have is a bad plan. Past generations worked to pay off their homes as quickly as possible. Today's masses have been repeatedly refinancing their homes to live.

Wise wealthy people shop for bargains and have to spend less than they make or they will erode their capital. One useful way to think about money is simply as a way to exchange energy. When we work for money, we invest our physical and mental energies and the resources of the planet in providing products or services for others. We then use the money received—now a token of expended energy—to exchange it for the products and services of others. Each time we are deciding to give money for something, we should consider whether it is likely to be a worthy exchange of energy.

The bottom line is that price should always matter. Price is the most important determinant of whether an investment is likely to be rewarding. If you pay too high a price, the odds of being rewarded drop significantly, but, again, this is the exact opposite to the way most people respond. Humans like to move in packs; they generally like to buy what they think everyone else is buying, so they pay premiums for name brands even where lesser-known brands are as good or better. When it comes to investing, people can be afraid of missing out, so when they see a particular asset has experienced large gains, they are attracted to it like bugs to a light. People want to buy more of what was a big gainer last year. The higher the price rises, the more they want in. The problem is, this impulsive tendency is exactly the wrong way to choose investments. Buying when prices are lower is the key to financial success. When prices are lower, there is a higher probability of the price going up from our entry point. Also, when we pay attention to price, we can develop rules about when to go against the pack and take our profits. In order to make money, we need to buy and then sell an investment, and using our gut to pick entry and exit points is a path to certain disaster.

Here is the trick to staying fit and healthy: eat less and exercise more. Here is the trick to retiring with money: spend less, save more. Both require living with self-discipline.

The truth about human nature is that it must be constrained in order to be wise. Even those of us who are educated and trained in managing money must guard against our human susceptibility to fear and greed. Unbridled optimism and rampant risk-seeking are well-worn paths to ruin when it comes to money. We have to set up objective rules to control our tendency to hubris, and we must act like grown-ups in taking responsibility for our money decisions. It is not easy to do, and it requires constant effort to maintain the discipline to protect us from ourselves and from the bad advice of others. But the truth can set us free.

Chapter 2
Benefiting from Market Cycles

Stock prices have reached what looks like a permanently high plateau. I do not feel there will soon be, if ever, a 50 or 60 point break from present levels, such as they have predicted. I expect to see the stock market a good deal higher within a few months.
—Irving Fisher, renowned Professor of Economics at Yale University, speaking Oct 17, 1929, just weeks before the Great Crash that saw the Dow lose 89% of its value over the next three years.

In order to understand investment markets, it is crucial that we acknowledge patterns in human behaviour. We must tailor our approach to investing to the market climate in which we find ourselves so we can make wise decisions. There is no one-size-fits-all approach that we can follow blindly. In the short term, world events are always changing with new risks and new opportunities cycling to the fore. Long term, human history tends to repeat itself. The one constant is the human dynamic that drives our behaviour and influences our decisions. If we are to avoid making classic errors with investing, we must study the long-term cycles known as secular cycles.

If the idea of studying capital market history seems repugnant, then I humbly suggest that you do yourself a great service: stop trying to invest. Buy some nice, reliable guaranteed deposit certificates at the local bank branch. You will fare far better over time with no market risk in a guaranteed safe approach than you will trying to invest without a certain level of understanding and self-discipline. There is no extreme makeover, instant solution to lasting financial success. It takes a daily commitment to learning, but lifelong rewards are well worth the effort.

Secular Cycles

The bull market in stocks from 1982 to 1999 was incredible. This was the best and smoothest bull in the history of world equity markets and was characterised by very low volatility and magnificent gains—about twice the 200-year average. Unfortunately, smooth sailing does not build the best sailors. Long periods of this can lull many into falling asleep at the wheel. When equities go so right for so long, they become a national obsession. Suddenly, risk is not being *in* the market, the risk is being *out*. But market cycles change. Over the past 100 years, there have been a series of very defined 20-year bull (up) and bear (down) cycles. We call these long 20-year trends secular cycles. During secular bull cycles, such as the ones from 1900 to 1920, 1940 to 1960, and 1980 to 2000, passively buying and holding stocks for the long term was a reasonable approach as stocks generally went up over the 20-year time frame. During secular bear cycles, such as the ones from 1920 to 1940 or from 1960 to 1980, however, buy and hold was a painfully unrewarding strategy with great interim volatility and low to no real returns.

Trumpeted by the investment sales industry, the habit of a static asset allocation—where a fixed weight in each account is perpetually allocated to equities—came to the masses through the smooth seas of the latest secular bull (from 1982 to 1999). Asset allocation targets came to shift more and sometimes entirely to equities. In the late '90s, there were some teams of Ph.D.s advising investors to embrace risk, telling them that anyone who understands anything about the markets would do nothing but passively hold stocks for the long run.

In support of the industry's interest in perpetually selling equities, the sales force latched onto the Gary Brinson study that concluded: "asset mix decisions account for 90% of a portfolio volatility."[6] Not surprisingly, the sales arm has long misquoted the study by saying instead that asset mix accounts for 90% of portfolio returns. This is the no pain, no gain mantra that encourages investors to be tough enough to ride out losing money in bad markets so they have a chance of reward in up markets. But the pain of loss is real and the hope of reward is just hope without the discipline we require to help us reduce price risk. We must keep in mind that a loss of 50% requires a subsequent gain of more than 100% just to recoup its value.

Jeremy Siegel is one of the poster guys for stocks for the long term. He wrote an impressive book entitled *Stocks for the Long Run* in the '90s. His research suggests that over a 200-year period, U.S. stocks have averaged 7% returns, which is better than bonds or cash. His message dovetailed nicely with the brokerage business in its purpose of getting people to buy equity products, and so many firms hired him to do client presentations and to train their teams of brokers. Then came the crash of 2000–2002 where many equity investors lost 50 to 80% of their invested capital. Undeterred, Siegel released an updated version of his book in 2003 where he reiterated his message and in the preface thanks the brokerage business for all their help and support in his career. Apparently, he has no shame in promoting the hand that feeds him.

The trouble with Siegel's thesis is that his 200-year time frame is largely irrelevant to mere mortals. The smoothed-out, long, long trend does not fairly reflect the experience of an average investor with a finite life span. To regular folks, 5-, 10-, and 20-year cycles matter most in their lives. Few people invest all their money with plans to look at it fifty or more years down the road. Most build their fortunes slowly over time, often with lumpy larger deposits in the later parts of their lives as they sell property, sell businesses, or receive inheritances. Investing in equities whenever there is available money, without regard to price and on the notion that stocks always go up long term, is a very risky proposition. Perpetually holding stocks is a hopeful strategy, not a cash-in-the-bank strategy. Realistically, we will eventually need to start using our savings for supporting our lifestyle at some point in our lives. And in the land of mere mortals, the price we pay for our investments and the price for which we sell those investments will always be highly relevant.

The 200-year 7% real average return that Siegel cites in stocks is, upon a closer look, comprised of more than 4% from the average dividend yield during the 200-year time frame and just over 2% from capital gains. When we compare that with today's environment, present average dividend yields of less than 2% are less than half of the historic average. Since stock prices today remain historically high, dividend yields are relatively low. If investors are to average 7% annual returns starting from present prices, they will need to see real growth in earnings and dividends of more than 5% per year or further expansion in the already very high price-to-earnings (PE) ratios in the market.

Realists must admit that the chance of a 5% or even 4% real annual growth rate in developed nations is slim to nil. Real annual GDP has averaged just over 3% for the past 100 years in the U.S. And real growth in corporate earnings and dividends has substantially lagged this growth in the overall economy. Real growth in corporate earnings has averaged about 1.5% per year, not anywhere close to 5% per year.[7] With average dividend yields of 1.5% and real earnings growth of 1.5%, the price investors are willing to pay for those earnings would need to expand considerably from current levels in order to reach 7% expected real returns per year. PE multiples are already at the third highest level in history, as the following chart from Robert Schiller depicts.

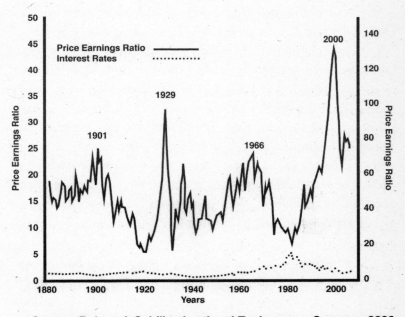

Source: Robert J. Schiller, Irrational Exuberance, Currency 2006

From present levels, a contraction in the price investors are willing to pay for earnings is more probable than a still further expansion. It is most likely that stock prices will either have to correct substantially from here or remain stagnant during the next several years in order for markets to average historic return levels.

While the long-term trend of a secular bear market is generally down or flat, within it, interim market cycles continue to follow the roughly 4-year business cycle, presenting several profitable trading opportunities (see historical Dow charts below). A productive strategy during secular bears is to buy near cycle bottoms and sell near cycle peaks. Once we exit equity markets, it is critical to wait in the safety and liquidity of cash in order to take advantage of lower prices as they present near the next cycle bottom.

If we look at the Andex charts investment salespeople love to show us (typically showing stock index performance over the last fifty years), we see a large-scale linear picture of a general increase in the price level depicted. But what is much harder to appreciate from these smoothed trend lines is the enormously wide swings the markets exhibit on either side of the long-term mean on a year-to-year basis. To appreciate the real-life experience, we need to examine price risk using logarithmic charts. Do you know the adage, "He who does not study history is doomed to repeat it"? How about, "Each generation's financial memory is exactly as long as their own experience"? Those who study market history can develop tools to profit from what it reveals about investor behaviour.

The following is a series of six logarithmic charts of the Dow Jones Industrial Average from 1900 to the present in 20-year segments. These charts and more are available through www.stockcharts.com and are complied through the insightful work of long-time analyst and respected market technician John Murphy.

Dow Index (1900–1920): A Secular Bull Market

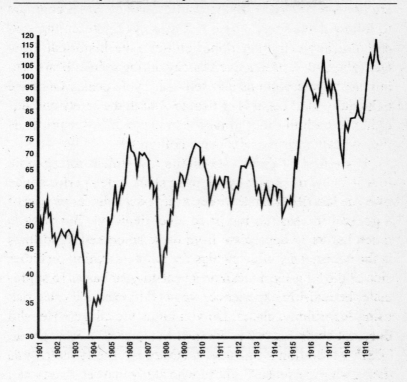

Source: www.stockcharts.com

During this first twenty years of market history, we can see that the general trend was that of a secular bull cycle. The trend was decidedly up from 1900 to 1920, although with considerable volatility. During this period, a buy-and-hold strategy worked reasonably well, provided one could endure the significant interim drops in the value of capital invested.

Dow Index (1920–1940): A Secular Bear Market

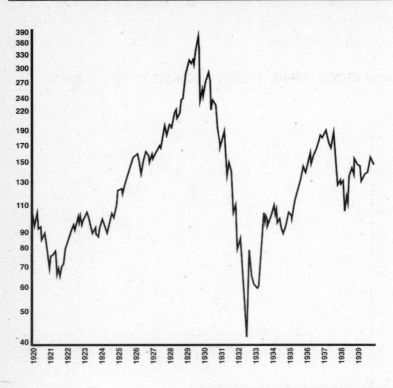

Source: www.stockcharts.com

This next period from 1920 to 1940 can be described as a cyclical bear market. The index started out on a dramatic uptrend, leading to the spectacular peak and debilitating crash of 1929 through 1932. Preceding this stock market fervour was another speculative run in real estate prices, particularly in Florida, where markets peaked and finally crashed in the fall of 1926. Undaunted, people who still had access to money turned their ambitions away from land to the stock market in increasing volume from 1926 through 1929.

Buy and hold over this 20-year period was a very unrewarding strategy, facing years of heart-pounding volatility.

For capital invested in this index at the market peak of 1929, it would take twenty-five years before prices were recouped. Most investors did not (or could not) hang on long enough to see their money recover.

Dow Index (1940–1960): A Secular Bull Market

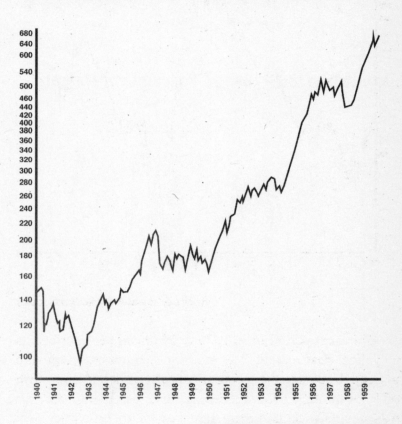

Source: www.stockcharts.com

The pain of the '20s was slowly forgotten as the next generation recovered from the Second World War and pushed forward with optimism for the future. This period from 1940 to 1960 can be characterized as the next secular bull market.

In 1944, the Bretton Woods conference established the U.S. dollar as the world's benchmark currency. While the rest of Europe dug itself out of the post-war rubble, the American economy surged with restored hope and initiatives to encourage education and home ownership through the G.I. Bill and other stimulative policies. Inflation and interest rates remained generally low for much of the period. Once again, buy and hold for investors was a rewarding and low-volatility strategy.

Dow Index (1960–1980): A Secular Bear Market

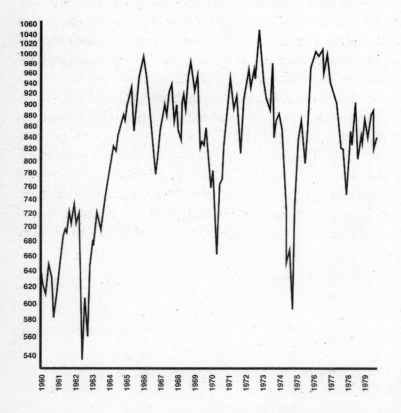

Source: www.stockcharts.com

The free-flowing capital and resultant spending of the '50s led to over-optimism and an inevitable correction in markets from 1960 to 1963. This ushered in the next secular bear market in stocks that lasted until 1982.

The '70s presented several themes reminiscent of present times with a U.S.-led war abroad, soaring commodity and energy costs, rising inflation, and a falling U.S. dollar. As pointed out by Peter Bernstein, "the intensification of the U.S. commitment to the war in Vietnam was the primary source of inflationary pressure" in the late '60s.[8]

Central bankers responded to unexpected levels of inflation with their standard tool—increasing lending rates—in an effort to contain a national habit of voracious consumption that was developed in the '50s. Once more, buy and hold was a painful approach for investors: low inflation-adjusted returns and high volatility over the 20-year period.

Of further significance during this period, in 1971, America removed the peg that attached the value of its dollar to an underlying gold standard. This paved the way for governments to literally print money at will. The habit has since persisted as a key strategy for funding apparently unlimited aspirations of many nations around the world. This has been particularly true in Canada and the U.S., where national deficits have now been a permanent feature for over thirty years.

Dow Index (1980 to 2000): A Secular Bull Market

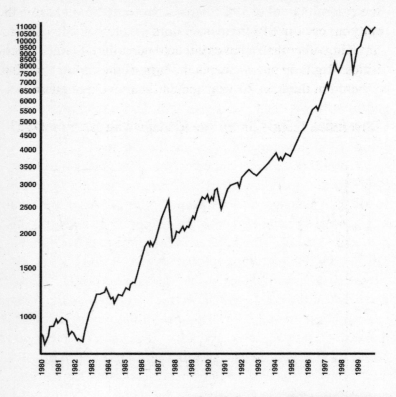

Source: www.stockcharts.com

This chart depicts the late great bull of the '80s and '90s, a time of incredible gains and extremely low volatility in this "new paradigm" of falling commodities, falling inflation, and falling interest rates.

People in the financial sales industry had a heyday during the '80s and '90s because they could perpetually sell equities and their customers were largely happy with the appreciation. So relentless were the market gains during this period that many mutual fund managers became intent on never allowing their funds to hold any cash. Cash not invested was returns not enjoyed. Holding any cash was considered "cash drag" likely to hurt a fund's performance. Risk became defined as the risk of not being in the market. Buy and hold became the rallying cry once more as investors questioned the need for anything other than a passively held portfolio of large cap equities. Right on cue, it seems the turn of the century in 2000 ushered in the next 20-year secular bear cycle in equities.

Dow Index (2000–2006): The Next Secular Bear Market?

Source: www.stockcharts.com

Here we see the likely beginnings of the next secular bear. A regular market correction started in March 2000 and was stretched into a two-year plummet with the attacks on the World Trade Center in September 2001. In an effort to avert global recession and jump-start consumption, governments around the world began to aggressively cut interest rates to levels not seen since the '50s. It took some time for consumers to start spending, but federal bankers ultimately prevailed and a new economic expansion got under way in 2003. In the U.S., the overnight lending rate was cut from its typical or neutral range of 5% down to 1% in 2003 (less than the rate of inflation) and it remained there for one full year! Finally, in 2004, the U.S. Central Bank began a long and gradual tightening track of quarter-point increases. By June 2006, the overnight rate was back at 5.257%. The expansion from 2003 to 2006 led to its usual symptoms of soaring commodity and energy prices, along with rising inflation. Meanwhile, consumer debt levels around the world climbed to record highs, with many North Americans registering zero and negative savings rates in 2005 and 2006. Market trends from the peak in 2000 to 2006 were highly volatile and low return for a buy-and-hold investor. Given the pattern of the past 100 years, this new secular bear could last until 2020.

Aggressive rate cuts successfully stalled a global recession in 2001. A significant economic slowdown was long overdue owing to excesses and overspending at the peak of the last expansion leading up to 2000. Low rates made money a cheap commodity in vast supply. This encouraged consumers to borrow money to spend on things they would not otherwise have been able to afford. There was apparently no incentive to save at all when cash in the bank was earning less than 2%. The downside of the reinflation based on widespread credit was that it effectively borrowed sales from the future to buoy profits and GDP in the present. In 2006, commentators praised record corporate profits. Considering the unprecedented free-flowing money of the previous five years, it should not be a surprise to anyone that profits appeared so robust. The anticipatory question was, how could they possibly continue such momentum?

The main support of the economy—the consumer—was

now drowning in debt for things acquired but not yet paid for. In a 2004 interview, legendary money manager John Templeton was already sounding concern on this front:

> The greatest threat to maintaining this level of economic activity is debt. There has never been a time when people worldwide, and especially in America, had such a high proportion of debt.[9]

A sage market analyst for over sixty years, Templeton has seen other periods in history where credit use became widespread. He has frequently cautioned that these trends tend to end badly. In the two years that followed his words, the trend to overspend using debt grew remarkably worse.

During secular bears, throwing capital into equities whenever you happen to have it or leaving equities passively invested have been high-risk propositions—lots of volatility and below average returns. From 1962 to 1978, buy and hold of the Dow 30 Index garnered a nominal annual return of just 1% capital growth over the entire 16-year period! That said, when we examine this time frame closely, there were in fact many rewarding trading opportunities within the secular cycle, provided one had a discipline to enter and exit the market.

Dow 30 (1960–1982): Trading Opportunities for a Timing Strategy in a Secular Bear Market

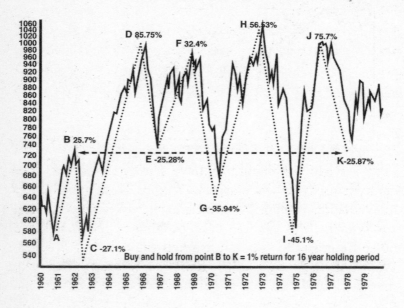

Source: www.stockcharts.com

Contrary to the uptrend of other world markets during 1982 through 1999, Japanese stocks laboured in a secular bear following the remarkable boom and then bust in Japan's economy and real estate markets after 1980. While the overall market was flat in Japan over this 20-year period, it too presented many attractive interim gains for a timing discipline to capture.

The Japanese markets being out of synch with other world markets was actually unusual during this period. Normally by virtue of global trade and the collective sentiment of humans on the planet, trends in world stock markets are remarkably correlated as shown in this chart of international indices during the market decline and recovery from 2002 to 2003:

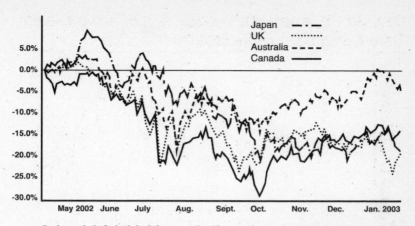

It is wishful thinking to believe that we can increase our equity returns in a bear market by simply reallocating money to international equities. When capital leaves North American equity markets at the peak of an economic cycle, it tends to do so in unison with public markets throughout the world. When human appetites turn against risk, we tend to flee risky markets like stocks and bonds in remarkable lockstep and turn to more risk-free assets such as cash and T-bills. The following chart of the Canadian TSX 60 index is virtually identical to the DOW chart from 2000 to 2006.

TSX 60 Canadian Index (2000–2005) Did a secular bear for equities begin in 2000?

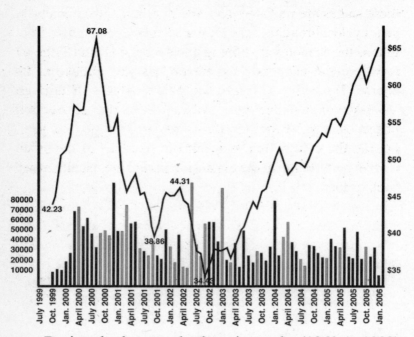

During the last secular bear in stocks (1960 to 1982), commodities, or hard assets, (gold, metals, and materials) outperformed paper assets (stocks and bonds). While high inflation is the enemy of stocks and bonds, it generally supports higher prices in hard assets. With its large weight in commodities, the Canadian market is a potentially good place to profit from the swings of a secular bull in hard assets over the next several years. But historically, price movement in commodities is highly volatile. There is a reason they are called "deep cyclicals." Commodities closely follow the rise and fall of the 4- to 5-year economic cycle. Profits can be made and retained where a timing strategy is employed with discipline. The hard reality: history tells us that a passive buy-and-hold approach is likely to be once again very unrewarding with high volatility and low returns.

The Economic Business Cycle

Respected market technician Martin Pring divides the economic business cycle into six stages. He points out that these stages are repeated over and over in approximately 4-year cycles throughout the longer secular trends. Stage I begins as the economy is slipping into a recession, and Stage VI is where the economic expansion has just about run its course. Typically, the expansion phase—stages III through V—lasts on average three years, while the contraction phase—stages VI through II—takes, on average, one year. During the contraction, one-third to one-half of the stock market gains made in the expansion period are usually given back or lost.

Idealized Business Cycle for the Six Stages of the Business Cycle

Stage 1	Stage 2	Stage 3	Stage 4	Stage 5	Stage 6
			Bonds ↓	Stocks ↓	Commodities ↓
	Recovery				
	Recession				
Bonds ↑	Stocks ↑	Commodities ↑			

Source: www.pring.com

Stage I:	Bonds turn up	Stocks and commodities fall
Stage II:	Stocks turn up	Bonds rise, commodities fall
Stage III:	Commodities turn up	All three markets rise
Stage IV:	Bonds turn down	Stocks and commodities rise
Stage V:	Stocks turn down	Bonds fall, commodities rise
Stage VI:	*Commodities turn down*	*All three markets fall—cash is king*

While the two years of falling stock markets from 2000 to 2002 was of longer duration than the historical average, in this next table we can see that large market declines are a regular occurrence throughout market history.

Market Cycles Defined by the S&P 500, Total Returns (%)

Expansion and Contraction in Markets

Up Markets: Expansion			Down Markets: Contraction		
Phase Dates	**# of mnths**	**S&P 500**	**Phase Dates**	**# of mnths**	**S&P 500**
Dec 1929 – Mar 1930	4	21%	Apr 1930 – Jun 1932	27	-80%
Jul 1932 – Aug 1932	2	92%	Sep 1932 – Feb 1933	6	-30%
Mar 1933 – Jan 1934	11	105%	Feb 1934 – Jul 1934	6	-21%
Aug 1934 – Feb 1937	31	135%	Mar 1937 – Mar 1938	13	-50%
Apr 1938 – Dec 1938	9	61%	Jan 1939 – Apr 1939	4	-6%
May 1939 – Sep 1939	5	22%	Oct 1939 – May 1940	8	-26%
Jun 1940 – Oct 1940	5	22%	Nov 1940 – Apr 1941	6	-13%
May 1941 – Aug 1941	4	14%	Sep 1941 – Apr 1942	8	-22%
May 1942 – May 1946	49	49%	Jun 1946 – Apr 1947	11	-21%
May 1947 – Oct 1948	18	23%	Nov 1948 – Jun 1949	8	-10%
Jul 1949 – Jul 1957	97	429%	Aug 1957 – Dec 1957	5	-15%
Jan 1958 – Dec 1961	48	105%	Jan 1962 – Jun 1962	6	-22%
Jul 1962 – Jan 1966	43	90%	Feb 1966 – Sep 1966	8	-16%
Oct 1966 – Nov 1968	26	52%	Dec 1968 – Jun 1970	19	-29%
Jul 1970 – Dec 1972	30	76%	Jan 1973 – Sep 1974	21	-43%
Oct 1974 – Dec 1976	27	86%	Jan 1977 – Feb 1978	14	-14%
Mar 1978 – Nov 1980	33	86%	Dec 1980 – Jul 1982	20	-17%
Aug 1982 – Aug 1987	61	282%	Sep 1987 – Nov 1987	3	-30%
Dec 1987 – May 1990	30	71%	Jun 1990 – Oct 1990	5	-15%
Nov 1990 – Apr 1998	90	345%	May 1998 – Aug 1998	4	-13%
Sep 1998 – Aug 2000	24	63%	Sep 2000 – Sep 2002	25	-45%

Annual gains experienced by a HOLD strategy over 20 years 1929–1949 = 3.8% per year
Annual gains experienced by a HOLD strategy over 12 years 1966–1978 = 4.1% per year

Expansion Phase Averages	**Contraction Phase Averages**
22 "Up Markets" 1926–2000	22 "Down Markets" 1929–2002
Average length: 31 months	Average length: 10 months
Average gain per cycle: 117%	Average loss per cycle: 26%

Source: Dimensional Funds

I recently came across a mutual fund newsletter from September 2002 that summarized the then state of affairs as follows:

The (grim) year that was: 2002 to the end of September. (Come on 4th quarter!!!)

The third-quarter drop on the Dow of 17.9% was the worst since the final three months of 1987, and its September decline of 12.4% marked the grimmest for the month since 1937!

September's decline puts it at six full months of decline on the Dow. For the year to date, the Dow is down 24.24%, the S&P is down 28.99%, the NASDAQ is down 39.9%, and the TSE is down 19.61%. The worst performing market in the world: Stockholm (down 46.7%), followed by the DAX (down 46.6%). This was all following double-digit declines in 2001. And now we enter October. According to the *Stock Trader's Almanac*, October is known as the Jin because of 1929, 1987, and 1997 plus 1978 and 1979, as well as Friday the 13th in 1989. However, October is also a "Bear" killer and turned the tide in nine post-WWII bear markets: 1946, 1957, 1960, 1962, 1966, 1974, 1987, 1990, and 1998. The worst six months of the year ends with October. Late October has historically been a great time to BUY equities over the years.

Q4 last year followed the nightmare of Sept 11, 2001 and was a complete wash for many businesses. As a result, Q4 2001 data should be pretty easy to beat, on a year over year comparison, which is how the market evaluates and looks for trends. From Q4 2000 to Q4 2001, the trend was a vertical drop, and this was reflected in the stock market of 2001 and

2002 to date. As a result, (barring any further large-scale tragedies), the Q4 2001 to Q4 2002 comparison should be a pretty startling jump up. This should give the markets a good kick-start into the winter of 2003.

As it turned out, October 2002 was indeed the bottom of the market contraction that started in 2000. For those who had the cash to invest in the fall of 2002, a very rewarding three and a half years followed to the peak of the economic expansion in 2006. For the capital that had remained passively invested throughout the crash of 2000 to 2002, the peak of 2006 was just getting back to where it had been six years earlier. The NASDAQ 100 was still down by over 50% from the 2000 high. It is interesting to note that although the above newsletter was correct in retrospect in encouraging investors to take advantage of timing and buy stocks in the fall of 2002, the same industry had urged investors to keep buying and not sell at the peak of 2000. At the end of the longest bull-run in forty years, the industry told people that market timing was not something one should do, even where investors had been incredibly overpaid. By encouraging people to stay fully invested in stocks and bonds throughout the business cycle, the industry dissuades investors from having money available to take advantage of discounted prices that inevitably become available at least once each market cycle. If we are to prosper, minimizing losses in the first place must be the central goal.

Public equity markets are in their essence an auction. Participants indicate their vote through the prices they pay to buy and sell. It takes a consensus of buyers over sellers in order to escalate a price. Once everyone who is likely to buy has bought, prices can rise no further. More sellers than buyers will drive prices down. Human behaviour creates our market cycles. Each generation has its own 20-year secular trend, and within those trends, we have shorter market/business cycles. We go from optimism to pessimism and back approximately every four years, roughly in synch with our political cycles.

The U.S. Presidential Cycle

As the world's largest consumer, the U.S., and its presidential cycle in particular, can perpetuate market cycles in North America and around the world. The theory goes like this. Incumbent governments want to be re-elected. In the year before and the year during an election, governments make promises and use the spin of future improvement to rally voter support. Once elected, their second and third years of the term are challenging because promising and delivering are two separate things. Promises are hope-based; their delivery is expensive and exacts an economic toll. A promised change forces unpopular decisions and cuts in other places. The honeymoon ends and the voters become disenchanted. Pessimism and fear become more broad-based. Consumers tend to consume less when their future seems negative. The economy and the stock market typically decline with their sentiment. By the fourth year of the term, promises start to fuel hope once again and the cycle starts over. Although growing population and wage trends support a gradual increase in consumption and GDP over the long term, in the intermediate term, GDP grows in the fits and starts of a business cycle. During the approximate three years of economic expansion, equity investments tend to increase in value; during the approximate one year of economic contraction, equity investments tend to drop in value. They frequently drop by a lot.

After eighteen years as Wall Street's top-ranked retail stocks analyst, Joseph Ellis offers the following advice about the need to navigate our way through the reality of market cycles:

... we must muster the courage to sell stocks when the year-over-year rate of change in consumer spending, at the front end of the cycle, is at its best, and optimism about the economy (i.e. encouragement to be heavily invested) is ubiquitous—or, conversely to wade into the market and purchase stocks when the world appears to be coming to an end.[10]

It is easier for brokerage analysts to make such honest suggestions about equities once they are retired and free to speak plainly, away from the mandate of the stock-selling firms that employ them.

Our firm attracts market-realist investors because our market timing approach appeals to those who have lived through real market cycles. In the spring of 2006, we sent our clients some charts showing the unusually high debt levels in North America after years of over-consumption fed by record-low interest rates. Our thesis was that such over-leverage would present problems for sustained increases in economic growth at the end of that cycle. In response, one of our clients forwarded the charts on to his adult daughters, who were successful executives in their own right, and had this to say to them:

Hi Girls,

These charts are excellent and they should be printed out and put in a file. We will discuss them at some future time and will be wondering how low prices can then go, and if they will ever hit bottom. I clearly remember the 1980s and that was the case. The top is reached when every last person who can be sucked in, is sucked in, and then it starts over again. It is sad as lives are ruined, marriages break up, and suicides rise. No, I am not exaggerating. Throughout my working history, I took advantage of every recession and economic downturn to buy assets for a fraction of their normal value. As you know, we made millions, and we will do it again. It takes patience, as every cycle goes to an extreme at the top and the bottom.

Dad

Chapter 3
The Truth about Asset Allocation and Return Expectations

*It is easier to be firmly anchored in the sea of nonsense
than it is to set out on the sea of meaningful thought.*
—John Kenneth Galbraith

Cash and its equivalents can be an important strategic asset class in a secular bear market. The discipline of holding cash at certain times can be crucial to financial success. When we are trying to cross a busy highway without a crosswalk, we must have patience. We must calmly wait at the side of the road while all the traffic roars past us. Only when the coast is clear can we venture safely to our destination on the other side. This is real-life investing without the sales hype. When no assets seem to be offered at discounted prices, cash, money market fund, and short-term bonds are the places to wait safely for things to come on sale.

Bonds and real estate can be excellent investments, but the same rules apply: if we pay too much for something, it will most likely turn out badly. The price we pay is our greatest risk. It may take years to recover invested capital; or worse, life events may force us to cash out before the prices come back. The longer the up-cycle goes on, the more complacent people become and the higher the risk that the price paid will be too high. Even with the remarkable real estate appreciation of the past few years, there are still properties today that could not fetch the price they sold for in the peak of the 1990 real estate frenzy.

Impatient and unenlightened clients can lose faith in portfolio managers who wait for buying opportunities. I am reminded of the brilliant horse trainer Ben Crane in the 2005 family movie *Dreamer: Inspired by a True Story*. The racehorse they have been working with has the promise of being a great champion and having a rewarding career, but on the day of the first race, he has a sore front leg. Crane tells the owner that the horse shouldn't race. The owner insists the race go on. Despite Crane's warning that participating in a race will put the horse at risk, the owner doesn't relent. Crane and the horse must do as he demands. The horse starts the race and collapses under a shattered knee joint a few seconds in. The vet says the horse is ruined and will never race again. Great potential was foolishly wasted. Experts with true discipline can only demonstrate their value when they are given the latitude and freedom to do their job. The emotions and impatience of others must not interfere if the manager is to deliver a service worth their fee.

Master investors don't seek to keep busy; they seek to wait patiently until an excellent opportunity matches their prescribed criteria. Waiting for the right investment at the right price is not a strategy well received by an investment industry paid to promote transactions. Most investment professionals are paid to come up with buy ideas. Fund managers are paid to buy things, not to sit in cash. This is the bias inherent in the system.

The best investors with sustained success over decades

all stress the need to wait in cash until true deals are presented. As Jim Rogers, former partner of George Soros, said, "One of the best rules that anybody can learn about investing is to do nothing, absolutely nothing, unless there is something to do."[11] This is also a sentiment that Warren Buffet has expressed many times over the years in his annual meetings and reports to the partners of Berkshire Hathaway. At the annual meeting of Berkshire in 1998, when equity prices were soaring past the moon, he said:

> We haven't found anything to speak of in equities in a good many months. As for how long we'll wait, we'll wait indefinitely. We're not going to buy anything just to buy it. We will only buy something if we think we're getting something attractive … We have no time frame. If the money piles up, then it piles up. And when we see something that makes sense, we're willing to act very fast and very big. But we're not going to act on anything if it doesn't check out. You don't get paid for activity. You only get paid for being right.

The rationale expressed in this quotation is logical, but few investors have the self-control to stick to the rules. Even where one intellectually understands the necessity for such an approach, it is typical for humans to have moments or days of weakness, or perhaps they catch *missingoutitis*. They grow weary of waiting. They just want to buy and get on with it.

For the rare managers who have a truly independent discipline to protect capital, it can still be hard to keep clients with you during the necessary periods of modest performance. The story of Foster Friess is one that sticks in my mind.

Friess was the founder and long-time manager of the Brandywine mutual funds in the U.S. During the bull market of the '90s, under his stewardship, the funds made fabulous gains in the exceptional equity markets of the time. Clients were very happy, but then prices went too far. Recall that the price-to-earnings ratio of the S&P 500 companies in the U.S. went from low single digits in the early '80s to above 20 in 1990 and then to a level never before seen in history: above 40 by the year 2000.

In 1997, Friess held an investment committee meeting with his team and asked that they scrutinize every security in the Brandywine funds and justify why they should continue to hold each asset in light of their incredibly high valuations. After objective scrutiny, the team acknowledged that most prices were well above rational metrics and at a high probability of a potentially major decline. They sold the vast majority of the equity holdings and parked the money safely in cash.

The correction in the fall of 1998 was heartening as it seemed to support that their analysis would be rewarded and cheaper prices would soon present themselves. But within a few months, equity prices rebounded again sharply and launched into the last and final leg of the incredible bubble in stocks. By late 1998, Brandywine funds were significantly underperforming the indexes and unitholders began to redeem their units in volume. Brandywine began losing millions of dollars in client capital weekly as investors rushed off to jump in with the hottest performing and fully invested funds. Finally, as assets under management shrank by half, Friess capitulated. They bought back into equities in 1999, just in time for the painful losses that began from March 2000 to October 2002.

In retrospect, Friess and company were not wrong to sell and lock in their incredible profits in 1997. They were early to leave, but they were not wrong. They were sticking to their discipline in their duty to protect the capital under their management. If they had waited for prices to correct, they would have been ideally positioned to step in and scoop up bargains, but since they seemed to be missing out on gains in the short-term, greedy and foolish clients concluded Friess had lost his touch. They abandoned his ship and jumped blindly into the perils of a bloated market just in time to lose heavily. Every good manager must miss out on some gains at the peak of each market cycle. Investors must prepare themselves to stick through these times in order to be ready to take advantage of the next inevitable downturn.

Portfolio Return Expectations

To understand realistic investment strategies, it is important to review some basic math about return expectations. Let's take the example of a typical balanced portfolio of 50% stocks and 50% bonds. If high-quality bonds are yielding 5% and long-term equity markets are expected to yield 7%, then the average expected return for the portfolio must be 6.0% per year less management fees paid.

Balanced Portfolio Reality:

50% bonds	X	5% =	2.5%
50% equities	X	7% =	3.5%
Gross expected portfolio yield:			**6.0%**

People with a balanced portfolio mix such as this will often say that they want a low-risk approach, while expecting returns of more than 10% per year! Many advisors seem oblivious to this math as well. Smart people set themselves up for certain failure if they don't train their expectations to reasonable return numbers. Keeping hopes in synch with reality is the key to making and following a rewarding investment strategy.

As explained in Chapter 2 on secular market cycles, if we hope to average 7% per year in equity returns over the next several years, it is likely that we will also need an objective discipline for buying and selling these assets. If our valuation rules indicate that equities are trading at very high prices, we need objective rules to tell us when to take that money off the table and wait in the safety of cash. If we are looking at our bond portfolio and it has made huge capital gains from falling interest rates, we need rules to tell us when it is time to take those gains and shorten the term of our bond holdings. Similarly, when every television show seems to be about home improvements and real estate is trading at multiyear highs because the masses have fallen madly in love with it, we must follow objective tests that measure price risk.

We can never afford to fall in love with an investment class. Nothing goes straight up forever, no matter what our heart or our neighbours may tell us. If we are investing in various assets with the same timing as the masses, we are likely to do poorly in the end. We must seek to arrive early at the party and leave before the end. We cannot be afraid to miss out on the last bit of fun, or we may overstay our welcome. Mature decisions are required and this means having rules and the discipline to apply them.

It is unreasonable to assume that we can leave every market right at the top and re-enter at the absolute bottom. If we do time our transactions this perfectly, it is mere luck. Many people hope that they will get out of a mania before it's too late, and yet, without an established plan, greed keeps the masses gorging at the table. Peter Bernstein aptly described the mindset that befalls investors who try to move forward by looking only at what has worked in the past:

"Yes," they think. "I won't get caught up in the next bubble, I'll get out sooner." But that's different from saying, "The basic investment structure that I've been using is no longer appropriate." That's a big step.[12]

Here, he is making reference to the reality of changing market cycles and the fact that the passive approach of the '80s and '90s is not likely to serve investors well in the present market cycle.

To be successful, a dramatic mind shift from past passive strategies is required. Realistically, we must set our valuation rules to leave before the masses do or we too will stay too late. Staying too late leads to painful loss. We have to leave earlier than most in order to be right, even though it may appear we are missing out. We have to look foolish before we can be shown to be wise.

Section II

The Spark:
The Sales Machine

Chapter 4
Beware the Investment Sales Industry

If you can't convince them, confuse them.
—Harry S. Truman

In May 2006, a major market contraction began in earnest all around the world. That same month, I witnessed the chief equity strategist for one of the larger U.S. brokerage houses being interviewed on Bloomberg television. Given the constraints of his role in the equity sales machine of his firm, he was refreshingly candid: "We believe there is a likelihood of a fairly significant market downturn over the next few months, so we are being conservative. We have increased our cash weight in our equity funds to 15%." "What about your own personal portfolio?" the commentator slipped in. "Personally? Well, personally, my cash weight would be around 40% of my portfolio." Interesting. The strategist was more defensive with his own money than the firm was recommending for its clients. Were interviewers to ask this of more of their guests, the exchange could offer greater insight for the viewers.

My first job in the financial services industry was with

an international securities brokerage firm and I am forever grateful for the education. Many honest people have started their financial career this way and have lived to tell the tale, but few can stick to it for long. Warren Buffett lasted for a year or so, and I lasted a long six. The father of value investing, Benjamin Graham, also started out with a brokerage firm in the early '20s. In those early days, there was no such animal as a stock or market analyst. People who were interested in doing mathematical calculations regarding the price of stocks were a fringe group known as statisticians.

At the time, one of the widely popular stocks was Consolidated Edison. Although the company was paying out a large dividend, it was widely rumoured to be distributing only a fraction of its available capital from interests it held in other ventures. Financial statements were not widely circulated back then and one did not have easy access to corporate data. Graham decided that he wanted to do some investigating into the "other ventures" of the company and visited the local city hall, where utility company financial information could be viewed.

After a few hours of careful analysis, Graham discovered that Consolidated was paying out all of its free cash flow to sustain the dividend at current levels and that the rumours regarding the company's other ventures were false. Amazed at his findings, a young and naive Graham hurried back to the brokerage house to inform his superiors of his findings. An elder mentor is reported to have taken Graham aside and rebuked him, saying, "Young man, it is people like you who are going to ruin this business!" Consolidated Edison went broke not long after Graham's revelation, taking the confident capital of many investors with it.[13]

I can strongly relate to the young Graham in this story. The brokerage business of the '20s was evidently much the same as the brokerage business that I found in the '90s. Arriving as a naive student, it took me a few years to realize how little stock promotion has to do with truth or the best interests of the firm's clients.

Large institutions play a vital role in maintaining liquidity in world markets and they play a crucial role in helping companies raise capital in world markets. But investors must never forget that the brokerage arms of these firms are the distribution channels for the firm's investment products through their sales force.

> Wall Street [and Bay Street] exist to sell investments.
> From a business point of view, no one on Wall Street
> has any earthly reason to ever suggest that the market
> is overpriced.[14]

As this quote reminds us, investment dealers make their money *selling investments to customers*. To make money, they need people to say yes and buy what they are selling. This has always been the case. There is little time spent training "advisors" on risk management principles. Where the job is getting people to buy products, counselling for restraint is counterintuitive.

In response to the need for independent risk management advice, investment counsel firms sprang forth to advise the wealthy on how to keep their money intact. This relationship provides a protective barrier between the unsophisticated investor and the security sales force. But as Ben Graham points out, once the sales force becomes disguised as "trustworthy advisors" with direct access to unsuspecting clients, a perilous imbalance takes hold:

> But a different situation obtains in a relationship be-
> tween the individual security buyer and the investment
> banking firms, including the stockbrokers acting as

underwriters. Here the purchaser is frequently inexperienced and seldom shrewd. He is easily influenced by what the salesman tells him, especially in the case of common stock issues, since often his unconfessed desire in buying is chiefly to make a quick profit.[15]

And so the sales culture of the financial industry feeds on the weakness of human nature and our common tendency to believe what sounds good. Investors must fortify themselves. They must not take their investment advice from salespeople. They must train their brain to reign in decisions based on greed and unreasonable expectations.

Greed breeds greed and sales firms get richer while individuals routinely lose money. In the past twenty years, risks to investors have compounded as larger firms bought up the smaller independents, making support of the mother ship's return on equity (ROE) the primary purpose.

The financial services industry spends millions of marketing dollars telling customers how smart, professional, and reliable it is. Clients are encouraged to trust and rely upon its expertise and advice. Herein lies the crux of the fiduciary gap. True professionals are held to a fiduciary standard of care for their clients. The courts have defined this standard over the years to include the following elements.

A fiduciary must:
1. act in the best interests of the client;
2. not make any secret profits out of their agency relationship; and
3. inform the client of any conflicts of interest.

The world of financial "advice" most often talks like a profession but walks like a self-serving sales force. True fiduciaries are not allowed to profit at the expense of clients.

They are not allowed to place their own pecuniary interests first.

When we buy toothpaste, we are buying a product. We expect that it will not cause our teeth to fall out and that it will generally help to maintain our dental health. But toothpaste manufacturers do not promise to advise us on our teeth and all other aspects of our health. We have dentists and doctors for that. The product provider does not assure us that they can be trusted to guide us through all of our complicated health issues. Unlike full-service investment firms, toothpaste manufacturers acknowledge that they exist to sell us just the product.

While investment firms are busy with expensive marketing campaigns to win the public's trust and confidence in "end to end" financial services, they are training their sales force on how to gain access to the clients' wallets. These two campaigns are inherently in conflict, and the clientele regularly pays the price. A recent article in the *Globe and Mail* reads: "Lost money on the markets, have you? The people at Goldman Sachs are very, very sorry about that. In fact, they are all crying as they count up their record $2.45-billion first-quarter profit. No, actually, they are laughing."[16] The cruel irony of these words leaps out. The sales firms make billions on the backs of unsuspecting buyers.

Some have asked why there are not more consumer protection laws in place in this area. Why has fiduciary duty played so small a role in financial advising to date while it has dominated other professions such as law and accounting? I will always remember the sense of awe I felt when I first toured the penthouse offices of securities firms. Priceless art and antiques furnished the lavish meeting and dining rooms. Here was where heads of state held regular consultation with the heads of international banks and big business. And who's in charge of protecting the little guy? Who is to make wise those who are required to have wisdom?

Those who spend more than they earn need to maintain excellent relations with their bankers. Over the past few decades, North American governments have become increasingly dependent on the kindness of lenders. Such support now forms the bedrock of our incredibly indebted nations. Spendthrift leaders are repeatedly elected to help the masses spend our way to prosperity. The majority is evidently not keen on electing fiscal restraint. A leader who suggests a life of restraint and paying down debt is, so far, unlikely to win the popular vote. The financial machine provides the products and the funding to support the vision of the have-mores. And so the vested interests favour the continued borrowing and spending of today without worrying about tomorrow.

Throughout history, there have been objective voices that have come forward in times of great positive consensus to advise caution to the masses. These individuals are usually scoffed at and scorned as being unpatriotic or too archaic to see the genius of the new times. No one likes to hear from a downer when everyone involved has much to gain by sustaining the status quo. The establishment has no interest in making investors doubt, and people believe best when they are most happy.

Writing in the '50s, Galbraith remembered first hand the blind optimism and reckless deployment of cash that preceded the crash of 1929 and the Great Depression that followed. He acknowledged that during such frenzied periods in history, there were many people who saw the looming dangers to the unsuspecting crowds:

Even in times of such madness as the late twenties, a great many men in Wall Street remained quite sane. But they also remained very quiet. The sense of responsibility in the financial community for the community as a whole is not small. It is nearly nil. Perhaps this is inherent. In a community where the primary concern is making money, one of the necessary rules is to live and let live. To speak out against madness may be to ruin those who have succumbed to it. So the wise on Wall Street are nearly always silent. The foolish thus have the field to themselves. No one rebukes them. There is always the fear, moreover, that even needful self-criticism may be an excuse for government intervention. This is the ultimate horror.[17]

And so the securities firms and the government leaders help each other retain power and wealth and the little guys are left to fare as they may. I find Galbraith's words enlightening because they underline just how remarkably little things have changed in this industry over the past 100 years. But also I am struck by how potentially more harmful this industry is in a modern era where workers are increasingly more responsible for funding their own retirement. Gone are the days when workers could blindly rely on their employers to provide them with guaranteed pension income. Now more and more workers are left to fend for themselves, falling on investment sales firms for desperately needed advice.

As investment firms and brokerages come and go, the expansion of the franchise is the predominant theme. At the opening of a new brokerage chain in our town, the big brass was flown in to address the open-house reception regarding the firm's big plans for adding new brokers and doubling the size of the sales force. Why they thought the attending clientele should be thrilled to hear about this is quite a mystery. A bigger sales force does not mean better service or advice, it just means more sales for the firm. Is it advice or is it sales? In finance at least, there is a conflict between these

two competing goals. Other professions have long understood the dangers of this conflict, but the investment advice
business remains wilfully blind.

One thing that originally attracted me to the financial
services industry was the notion that it was another type of
profession. It made sense that people needed an advisor who
knew about money matters as their specialty. I knew first-
hand that most lawyers and many accountants knew very little about investing, so how would one get good advice in
these matters without consulting a financial professional?

The barriers to entering the financial services "profession" are quite low and so all walks of life market themselves
under that title. Some candidates have undergraduate degrees
in something and they are generally the ones scooped up by
the firms that offer the best benefits and perks. The brokerage
sales force tends to be better regulated than the smaller mutual fund franchises, but the educational requirements to enter
the sales force of any of these institutions are generally low.
If people join from the life insurance side, they often have
written a couple of short exams on their products. If they
come from the mutual fund sales side, they may have written
the same exams and maybe a financial planning exam or two.

Basically, all of this "expertise" can be gained without rig-
orous testing or intellectual commitment, often within a few
weeks or months. This is the first problem in the financial advice industry. Standards that are too low allow for advisors
with nothing more than a general understanding of financial
concepts or the products they are trained to sell. Another problem is that the industry tends to attract people who are interested in making large commissions without having to do much
work, as there is little time commitment and discipline required to enter the sales force. Although education level isn't
a measure of ethical integrity, where there are fewer filters on
who gets in, there tends to be lower-quality candidates. Most

people are attracted to professions on the expectation that they will develop a specialty and make above average compensation for their work. But masquerading as a professional in financial sales can earn you a lot of money if you are a good talker. Smooth talkers are attracted to the industry in droves, especially at various peak times in the markets.

The sad reality is that the financial advice market has long been populated by some of the most tenacious salespeople around. They convince countless gullible people to leverage their home equity and buy mutual funds or all kinds of insurance products and limited partnerships. People are cross-sold every possible product, including antique coins and Arabian horses, all delivered with the skill of a seasoned boxer and his one-two punch. There are many problems that flow from this scenario. First of all, people end up with a plethora of financial products that are most beneficial to their sellers. Most of the fees are internally charged or are "hidden" commissions, so the customer has no concept of how much money their advisors are making for their "advice." Good sales reps are able to talk people into just about anything. Gobbledygook credentials sound impressive to the average person. Vulnerability is compounded since many consumers feel uncomfortable and ignorant about money matters. And just as with U.S. elections, candidates who can spend enough money on an advertising campaign buy a certain aura of "expertise" that resonates with wide audiences.

One of the classic examples of what is wrong with the industry is when "advisors" advertise their various sales awards. It looks impressive when your real estate agent is acknowledged as being excellent in sales—that's a good hire for selling your house. But why anyone would want to work with financial advisors renowned for their sales abilities is beyond comprehension. Weren't you looking for unbiased advice?

In the '40s, long-time Wall Street trader Fred Schwed, Jr.

wrote a gruff little book called *Where Are the Customers' Yachts?: or A Good Hard Look at Wall Street*. His title perfectly sums up why a rational person would not want to get investment advice from firms that earn money by selling investments to their customers.

One need only note the ads for financial service jobs to see the focus of the occupation. A typical ad reads: "Are you highly motivated, looking for a financially rewarding career? Become a financial advisor. No experience necessary, training provided." Despite what you may think, no law is being broken. There is no demanding code of ethics regulating this. Short of outright theft and embezzlement, all is fair in love, war, and investment sales. The industry feeds upon the weaknesses of human nature and clients play a large role in their own poor results. Like their advisors, clients are frequently looking for short cuts to easy street. To get there, they will accept a ride with the drivers who offer to get them there the fastest or who drive the flashiest car. If more attention were paid to the safety features, planned routes, and driving experience, most people would fare better.

The Analysts

After a couple of years working on the sell side of a brokerage firm, I had to admit that I knew nothing about managing risk to capital. All the training and courses I had taken to that point had focused on product basics and sales concepts.

The real experts in a brokerage firm are said to be the analysts in head office. They are there to do the analysis and download their genius to the sales force in the form of recommended lists. One day it hit me as I was reviewing one of these lists and noticed that there were 295 "buys" or "strong buys" and only 5 "reduce" or "neutral" recommendations on all of the stocks in the firm's universe. How could this be? If all the companies were a buy, then no one would need to sell—ever. What about the business cycle? What about the fact that equity markets repeatedly went through periods of sharp and prolonged declines? Stock prices generally follow the business cycle: they go up in anticipation of improved earnings during an economic expansion and they drop in anticipation of reduced earnings during an economic contraction. Yet, according to our experts, most stocks were always a buy. I decided that I needed to become an analyst to examine this further. I started the Chartered Financial Analyst (CFA) program, studying before and after work each day. It was as though I had bounded down the rabbit hole. Once I started, there was no going back.

What I discovered was that the analysts do not have nearly all the answers for a couple of reasons. First, like psychics, they essentially try to discern the future by looking at elements of the present and the past. This is a difficult task, to be sure, and one that calls for humble honest analysis that goes for the highest probability shot to avoid great dangers. Analysts are mostly intelligent hard-working people, but in many cases, their reach for the brass ring has taken them to working for big firms with a set agenda: to sell people investments. To foster perpetual sales growth, one has to look on the bright side and figure out ways to pump sunshine 24 hours a day.

Prudential Securities is one of a few international securities firms that does not have an investment banking department. Free from the restrictions of corporate underwriting, Prudential's analysts rank the prospects of a company as they see them instead of buckling under the pressures of management. Michael Mayo is a sell-side analyst who now works at Prudential. In twenty years at four of the largest brokerage firms in the U.S., he tells how he was often reprimanded and even dismissed for reporting honest analyses that ranked companies as sells. Mayo was the only Wall Street analyst to testify before the U.S. Senate Committee on Banking, Housing, and Urban Affairs as part of the Sarbanes-Oxley Act that proposed stricter rules for corporate governance in this area.

Even so, Mayo notes in his May 2006 article "Why Independent Research Is Still Rare" that notwithstanding the fallout and attention to this issue after the market crash in 2000, analyst impartiality has not improved: of the 10 largest U.S. stocks by market capitalization, there were 193 buy rankings and only 6 sell ratings. Mayo goes on to explain that even working at an independent such as Prudential does not prevent an analyst from suffering backlash for honest calls. Corporate management will often refuse to speak to analysts who rank their company a sell, blocking them from timely information that buy-ranking analysts enjoy. Other times, the analysts are harassed and threatened:

> We still find ourselves the object of formal, and sometimes threatening, complaints from management and/or their attorneys alleging bias, inaccuracies, and/or securities violations. It might not surprise you to learn that in 100 percent of such complaints (six to twelve a year, on average), the analyst's ranking was unfavourable. After extensive investigations by compliance, legal, and, occasionally, outside counsel, we have never found a basis for any of the accusations except for inadvertent inaccuracies that were generally immaterial to the analyst's investment case. We believe that this pattern of "complaint" is nothing other than thinly veiled intimidation aimed at analysts expressing independent investment opinions.[18]

From this we see that even where analysts are trained to give their professional opinions on valuations, and even where they work at independent firms, the vested interests of investment sales and banking seek to dominate and direct their conclusions. And when it all comes crashing down, as it ultimately always does, the analysts are criticized for ranking stocks a strong buy while prices plummet. At the bottom of the cycle, many are fired and reshuffled among the larger firms, poised to begin anew once the next uptrend begins.

Each securities firm usually has a couple of "old guys" in the wings who can help with their PR and assure people that over their thirty or fifty years of market experience, they have seen it all and stocks always work out. Their words of long-time experience carry a lot of weight for some and this can make their message all the more damaging when taken to one's portfolio.

In the spring of 2000, just after the NASDAQ was about 15% into its two-year slide to negative 80% returns, one of the "old guys" was marched out to a brokerage-sponsored luncheon I attended. Clients and prospects of high net worth had been invited to hear some sage words. Unfortunately, the sage, despite all of his market experience, was short on wisdom but quite long on stocks. He assured people that recent 10 to 15% declines on some of the tech stocks was merely a buying opportunity pullback. He suggested that names like C-MAC and Nortel should be scooped up at around $80. It made sense. If these stocks were a strong buy at $100 and $120 (as the analysts had confirmed), then long-term investors had a bargain at $80.

This sage carried extra weight because of his age and time in the business. The audience seemed very impressed. In the two years following his "buying opportunity" speech, C-MAC went bankrupt and Nortel went to $0.67.

There was a host of star analysts that became famous during the latter part of the '90s as the stock market staged its most incredible rally in history. Jack Grubman, Mary Meeker, and Henry Blodgett were just a few of the U.S. celebrity analysts who garnered an enormous international following. All worked for the major selling houses and all had prolific falls from popularity once the market declines were widespread. Some, including Grubman, were hauled off to jail, others, such as Blodgett, were simply taken out back and fired.

Dan Reingold was a top-rated telecom analyst on Wall Street through the '90s, when the deregulation mania was taking the world by storm. The underwriting firms were charging astronomical fees to help companies merge, acquire, and go public. After retiring in 2003, Reingold released his own memoir of the times, *Confessions of a Wall Street Analyst: A True Story of Inside Information and Corruption in the Stock Market.* The book gives vivid insight into the nepotism of governments, bankers, brokers, and company executives. He points out that in the current system, the odds are horribly stacked against outsiders and individuals trying to passively invest in publicly traded companies with any success. In the end, he cites the "painful truth," which he says individuals must accept: they should not be buying individual stocks because there are too many insiders with too many unfair advantages.[19]

In 2003, after the crash, when Maggie Mahar was writing her excellent account, *Bull! A History of the Boom, 1982–1999,* she tracked down Henry Blodgett and interviewed him about his time in the limelight. She describes a much-humbled Blodgett sitting with her in a coffee shop in New York.

> "Have you ever read John Galbraith's *A Short History of Financial Euphoria*?" he asks. "Every cycle the market looks for a hero to lead them through a euphoric peak, someone of average intelligence is made into a genius." Blodgett raised his hand. He almost yawns as he lays it out for you.[20]

In the history of humans and market cycles, our behaviour is evidently timeless.

Ben Graham became the founding father of the Chartered Financial Analyst (CFA) degree in the '30s because he saw the need for people to be trained to conduct objective measurements that help investors understand and determine which investments are likely to present value. He was also a finance professor for many years where he taught many of the then Wall Street statisticians. It is not that financial analysis has no merit, it is that the tool becomes a dangerous weapon where it is used only to support the presupposed thesis that stocks are always a good buy and risk is always your friend. When conventional metrics such as price-to-earnings ratios go off the charts at the peak of market cycles, the masses pile into the popular trends and the big firm analysts must seek other tools of valuation. EBITA (earnings before interest, taxes, and amortization) became the measuring tape in 1999 when earnings *after* taxes, interest, and amortization were too weak to justify market prices.

Technical Analysts

Technical analysts are trained to follow market prices, volume, and breadth to assess values relative to historic data. They too must be careful if their tools are to be of benefit. Confident predictions about the future are dangerous, and pattern recognition can be highly subjective. But it doesn't take a secret decoder ring for one to look at a chart and determine whether prices are historically high or low. If you add capital during 4- to 5-year highs, there is a higher probability of loss. Like golfers, an enlightened investor must look for the highest probability shot rather than confident forecasts.

In my view, technical analysts are a bit of a skeleton in the closet for big dealer firms. Where technicians stick to the discipline of their charts, they will uncover buys, but they will also find sells! Sells are not productive in the culture of buy, smile, and wave. Brokerage firms may have a technician or two kicking about the building, but mostly they are called on to help stimulate short-term trading ideas to generate some commissions and to manage the risk of the firm's own portfolio, not the portfolios of their perpetually buying clients.

My partner, Cory Venable, is one of the finest technicians I know. He does not have all the answers but he has a lot of tools to keep us off the shoals. At our independent firm, we use technical analysis to help determine buy and sell points for our investment universe as a major tool in our duty to manage risk to client capital. Every so often someone will express surprise that our firm uses technical and fundamental analysis to manage money. Aren't the two camps mutually exclusive disciplines? they will ask.

Managing risk to capital is such a large task; we see wisdom in using all the tools available. Many of the current Chartered Market Technician (CMT) students are people who were originally trained as fundamental analysts. In the last long bull market, risk management tools fell by the wayside because risk was low and average 5-year returns were incredibly high. Ed Easterling, author of *Unexpected Returns: Understanding Secular Stock Market Cycles*, calls this period a time when one could just hoist some pulleys and sail. But during cyclical bear markets that follow these days of high winds, Easterling points out that we need to row. Rowing is hard work. It means having rules and discipline to protect and grow capital. Humble discipline, not salesmanship, is required.

The Online and Discount Brokers

Large banks and brokerage firms have set up many online trading companies in the past decade. Online trading generates excellent revenues for them, but not for their customers. Casinos and online brokers have quite a lot in common: they both advertise to attract the addictive side of human nature, and both take no responsibility for the outcome to their customers.

During the latter part of the '90s, online brokers became the most advertised service on network business channels. Ad after ad dared people to have the courage to hit the button: buy, sell, buy, and sell, all at lightning speed, as if the speed of the transaction had anything to do with success as an investor. Machismo in investing was encouraged, regardless of age or sex. As the tech stocks soared out of the stratosphere, more than ever, people were sucked into the marketing machine. The path to great wealth was but a click of a mouse button away while you ran a bath, cooked supper, or visited with friends. Information—buckets and buckets of it—was sold as key knowledge needed for success. All you needed to do was read the reports available online and you would have the inside scoop.

During market peaks, waves of excited investors spring up all over. (We have also seen the same phenomenon in overzealous real estate markets.) Housewives and business-people alike are encouraged that they can be "plugged in." Thanks to online information, they can figure out investing themselves in just minutes a day. Why pay anyone for advice when the truth is given free with your online trading account?

The ability for people to make split-second decisions about investments based on split-second information is more likely to be hazardous than beneficial to one's financial health. At best, this feeds into the neurotic human tendency to be rash, impatient, and emotional. By focusing attention on the cheapness of the transaction commissions, the online brokers distract their customers from any of the larger issues that matter most, such as what they are doing, why, and at what risk. And then there are all of the transaction costs that the online customers are not aware of, such as the bid/ask spread, timing costs, exchange rates, and other snippets of profit that the institutions are able to shave off the capital as it races from click to click.

After the market crashed in March through September 2000, ads for the online traders fell off dramatically. Like a drug pusher who has exhausted the resources of his customers, they faded back into the shadows to await the next big frenzied opportunity. As markets re-tested the 2000 highs in 2006, I noted the number of online ads growing once again. A recent ad had a woman coming back from a jog and clicking a trade at the kitchen counter as she gulped down a refreshing drink. Mindful investors ought to see these ads as red flags. Controlling your emotions and sticking to your rules is much harder in practice than it sounds in theory. Those who can execute their strategy with calm and discipline will always be a rare and valuable commodity.

Chapter 5
Mutual Funds and Management Fees

The national public interest and the interest of investors are adversely affected...when investment companies are organized, operated, and managed in the interests of the investment advisers, rather than in the interest of shareholders.
—Investment Company Act of 1940, Preamble

In the early '20s, the forefather of mutual funds—the investment trust—came to the United States, having been around since the 1880s in England and Scotland. The structure was conceived as an everyman's vehicle for accessing equity investments. People with small amounts of money could add them to one collective pot, thereby warranting professional managers. This was a good idea at its inception. It reflected the notion that individuals with limited finances needed more diversity of holdings than their capital could afford. The concept of not having all your eggs in one or two baskets made good sense. Less company-specific risk meant less chance of permanent capital loss. It was the first chance at risk management regular folks could afford.

During the later stages of all bull markets, the popular

consensus is that stocks are only going up; therefore, no sell strategies are advised. If an investor needs to take money back, they simply sell their units at the market price or redeem them through the fund.

In the stock market bubble of the late '20s (and '90s), the investment trusts became sites of enormous hubris on the part of the companies who created them. Anytime you have marketing companies collecting substantial hidden fees from unitholders who do not see what they are paying nor understand what they are getting for it, there are great opportunities for abuse of trust. And so long as gains are big, unitholders are happy to not question much, especially when bull markets have gone on for longer than average. When markets are good, overconfidence and complacency remain at the fore.

Investment counsel firms are retained to manage mutual funds. They are highly trained discretionary portfolio managers entrusted with the fiduciary duty of managing the hard-saved capital of the fund unitholders. So far, so good, you may say, except that human nature, inspired by the greed of large numbers, rears its ugly head. Enter the marvellous marketing document, the prospectus. The prospectus is meant as a document of constraint. It sets out, among other things, what the managers can invest in, how much leverage they may use, and how much of the capital in the fund can be held in the various asset classes of cash, fixed income, and equities.

There is a significant bias in the money management industry where companies are paid higher fees to manage a portfolio of equities over fixed income or cash. The rationale is simple enough. If bonds are expected to earn 5% and cash is expected to earn 3%, then a 2 to 3% management expense fee seems intolerably rich for unitholders. The fees would all but consume any benefit they stood to gain. However, if equities can be expected to gain at least 10% per year, a 3% fee seems more reasonable. Volatile sectors such as energy or technology may be expected to return even more than 10% (depending on one's timing) and thus such specialty funds can be set up to charge even more. So in the interests of maximizing fees, funds are established with prescribed equity mandates such as U.S. growth, U.S. telecom, Canadian resources, or Canadian large cap value. Many of their policy statements stipulate that the portfolio managers can never hold more than a fixed small percentage of cash, often less than 10%.

Investment constraints are supposed to help limit risk, but these limitations in a prospectus actually serve to increase market risk to capital. Why? Because they dictate to portfolio managers that even if Canadian resource stocks have gone up an unsustainable 100% in the past two years, managers must keep fully invested and just keep buying them with the monthly inflow that salespeople keep sending their way. Even in generic, supposedly broad-based equity funds, if a couple of high-flying stocks in an index have been bid up to nose-bleed levels, managers who are mandated to track the performance of that benchmark will overweight the same companies in their funds in order to track the performance of the index. They do this notwithstanding the added price risk that this allocation inflicts on their capital under management.

Good money managers must have a buy-and-sell discipline with objective rules that determine whether they can add new capital to a certain investment and when it is prudent to collect profits and sell. As we saw in the previous chapter on market cycles, there are periods to be in certain markets and there are periods where it is best to be out of those markets altogether. Just imagine the horror (or what should have been horror) of technology fund managers in the late '90s. Their sector returns had been off the charts and the mutual fund sales force kept bringing them escalating new deposits each month. Lemming-like investors are most eager to send capital into bubbles right at the peak. Even if nothing appears as good value, mutual fund managers are generally constrained by their mandate to keep shovelling cash into the fire. If conventional valuation rules are unable to signal a buy, managers are required to change the rules, pick new metrics, and figure out a way to keep on buying—and so they do. Investors repeatedly pay a heavy price in mind-numbing losses to hard-saved capital. This will continue to happen as the mutual fund industry depends on salesmanship over independent risk management.

The irony is that for money managers, the smaller the assets, the more nimble the execution. The larger the asset pool under management, the harder it is for a manager to enter and exit particular holdings without bidding the market prices of your holdings against the fund. Elephants are cumbersome and less efficient in this area. John Bogle and others have long lobbied regulators to curb the marketing arm of fund companies from attracting more and more assets without concern for the cost to existing unitholders:

> Growth in a fund's assets to elephantine size enriches managers but destroys the fund's ability to repeat the performance success that engendered that very growth. The bigger the fund, the bigger the fee, and the more likely the fund's reversion to the market mean.[21]

Here, Bogle was speaking to the U.S. Senate Government Affairs Subcommittee in 2003. Legislators have been alerted to the dangers of the current system many times over the years. Unfortunately, they have thus far lacked the political will to make changes.

The underlying premise of mutual funds is that the average person has little understanding of how to invest and lacks the knowledge of what basic principles are important. On top of this, even if people do have an understanding of these fundamentals, they often lack the discipline to consistently manage their investments in a systematic and risk-adjusted manner. Unfortunately, although the mutual fund managers theoretically possess the knowledge and understanding of the rules and strategies involved, other competing agendas prevail as the sales arm puts its own interests ahead of all else. This is quite simply a breach of the fiduciary duty of care that professional managers owe to their unitholders. But this is the way the money world works.

The fund industry today seeks to sell people on the idea of being continuously invested—"Don't expect to take your money back out of the fund for at least five to seven years"; "Don't look to time the markets but rather leave the investment decisions up to the portfolio manager." The unitholder is directed to passively hold the units and not second guess the manager's strategy.

To help retain invested capital, the fund companies developed the concept of back-end loading sales commissions, or DSC (deferred sales charge). Like a barb on a fishing hook, this back-end fee is designed to keep an investor on the hook. If they wriggle off within the first five to seven years, they are dinged for amounts starting at 5% of the initial investment amount. This serves to cover the 5% commission the mutual fund paid upfront to the salesperson who placed the client's money in the fund to begin with. It takes rich fees to richly compensate all of the levels of marketing and administration needed to run mutual fund sales. Keeping funds in the market is the necessary prerequisite to keeping fees rolling in, and so market history is selectively snatched and captured in glossy brochures to support the buy-and-hold thesis and the industry's own ambitious growth plan.

Buy and hold has been marketed as the antithesis of

speculation, and perhaps for that reason, any attempt to cash out an investment is deemed dangerous—one might miss out on a couple of the best return days! Buy and hold for mutual fund holders is sound logic if the portfolio managers were actively managing the fund into and out of equities, but, as we have seen, the investment world is a complicated place where all of its salespeople are paid most when they are long in the market. True risk management parameters can get lost in a world driven by the marketing prospectus. There is a tendency to lose focus on the little guys and their finite life spans when you are busy wielding great wealth with great theory and confidence.

Management Fees

Many of the financial planning books that have been written in the past decade use double-digit return numbers for their retirement projections. A typical rate has been 10 to 13% per year. This myopia is based on the unusual experience of the '90s. But in a secular bear market with lower stock market returns, we must adjust our equity expectations to more reasonable targets. This is a time when scrutiny of the fees investors pay becomes extremely important. When rates of return are at 15%, 3% per year in fees may not seem bothersome, but when expected returns are at 6%, a 3% fee is untenable. Fees will necessarily matter more in the decade ahead than in the decade past. Reduced management expenses, both in management fees and marketing dollars spent, will be needed to secure reasonable investment returns for investors.

Starting in the '70s, John Bogle revolutionized the Vanguard group of funds in the U.S. by moving the management company from this fee-heavy model to a passive index system that slashed fees to cost. With his many articles and books over the years, Bogle is among those who have strongly criticized the fund industry for its voracious consumption of client capital and its refusal to pass on to unitholders the savings that inevitably flow from economies of scale. As the funds collect more assets, their profit margins are higher, meaning the fees charged to clients should go down, not up. Yet, this does not appear to be happening. Clients who invest millions of dollars often pay the same high fee percentage as those who invest a few thousand dollars.

At the end of the day, investors without the expertise or desire to be a do-it-yourselfer must pay for professional portfolio management. The question is, what is a fair and transparent fee for the service? Some of this will be dictated by asset size. As in other areas, economies of scale should afford the customer better rates. As a client has more funds to invest, they should pay a lower management rate. As a manager gathers more assets and enjoys greater efficiencies of scale, they should be expected to lower management fees charged to a fund. Any company with insatiable aspirations for assets under management should be looked at with scepticism when they profess devotion to their clients' best interests.

In money management, as in other services, keeping fees transparent and accountable is the only reasonable approach. It helps keep the industry honest. This rationale forms the basis for the U.S. House Bill H.R. 2420, the Mutual Funds Integrity and Fee Transparency Act of 2003, which calls for the fund companies to report a dollar amount per thousand that investors pay in expenses for the year. To go further, this calculation should be applied not just to hypothetical amounts but also to the clients' actual account balances, and this information should be listed on their account statements each year. Only in this way can clients truly know exactly how much they have paid to their management company in a year. Only then can they assess the value of the fees paid. Not surprisingly, the industry to date has been heavily opposed to this type of transparent reporting of fees, but those who oppose truth and disclosure must be boldly overcome if money management is to be an accountable and respectable profession.

Fees matter. Even if an all-equity fund is successful in averaging 8% per year in returns, fees of 2.75% per year will consume more than 57% of the benefit to the client over a 20-year period.

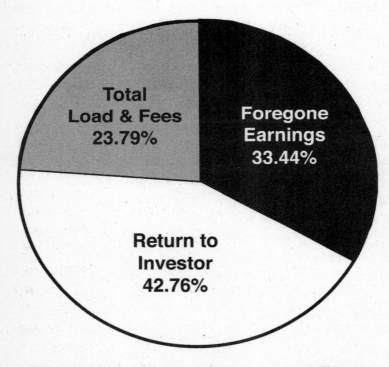

What do I keep of the growth on my money? The answer is less than 43%!

Source: www.investored.ca

Chapter 6
Fundamental Analysis and Stock Prices

Hope is a good breakfast, but a poor supper.
—American proverb

During the fiscal years 1999 through 2000, General Electric (GE) enjoyed solid earnings growth of 13.3%, or roughly 6.2% per year. Over the same time frame, its annual net income increased 18.8% for 1999 and 7.5% for 2000; meanwhile, its common share value rose a whopping 152%! What a fabulous reward from this "low risk" stock. Many wondered where the incredible multinational could be headed next, and in the period that followed, the company's net income continued to grow an average of 5.7% per year from 2001 through to the end of 2003. The stock value, however, dropped more than 60%. Throughout this time, GE was rated low risk and ranked a "buy" to a "strong buy" by most investment houses on the street.

Corporate officers have a large vested interest in having their companies and their shares well received, marketed, and taken up by investors. Their character, pride, and fortunes are dependent on it. Companies pay huge underwriting fees to brokerage firms to retain their sage assistance in implementing this task. Amid such great momentum of will and aspiration, there is little tolerance for pessimism and caution. Money managers looking for investments are trying to get a comprehensive read on each business. All the promoters and inside players have a natural interest in keeping to themselves the negative aspects about the business wherever possible. Corporate earnings follow the ups and downs of the business cycle. Since investors and analysts prefer smooth trends and stable dividends, management has an inherent mandate to smooth out earnings—this means being creative with their business plan and financial statements.

The officers who are trained to take the measurements and draft the reports, naturally adjust the results to fit management's desired thesis. The numbers are supposed to be objective and above reproach but they can be highly manipulated. Extreme examples of dexterity can be recalled from the peak and crash of the late '90s: Tyco, Adelphia, WorldCom, Kmart, Nortel, and Enron (end-run). Off-book accounting measures and outright fraud were creatively glossed over in annual reports. When performance numbers no longer look good through traditional ratios of net income and revenue, management and sell-side analysts are deft at developing new ways to characterize and present the information. The public will buy anything properly marketed. This is how companies with enormous financial losses can be touted as good investments and trade for hundreds of dollars per share.

In 2001 and 2002, as financial experts and executive officers were called up on charges one after the other, I was repeatedly reminded of *The Wizard of Oz*, when the curtain is pulled back and the little man pulling the strings is revealed as a fraud. Everyone gasps in horror, yet why didn't anyone notice this earlier?

Fundamental analysis is a legitimate discipline requiring

significant training and skill. However, its utility to investors remains dependent on the assessment of historical information that is filtered and carefully constructed by accountants, management, and promoters hired to help sell the story. Even in the absence of fraud, getting to the bottom line through financial analysis is no easy task. Even when we can get a true assessment, company shares rarely trade for their "fundamental" worth for more than a few fleeting moments in time.

One must come to terms with some basic truths about the market and its movers. The stock market is an auction. As Benjamin Graham and David Dodd said, it is a voting machine, not a weighing machine. The auction is populated by participants governed partly by reason and partly by emotion. If the auction were governed by accountant-robots it would be a much more boring but rational place to do business. Long-time top-ranked telecom analyst Dan Reingold (now also retired) says the markets are and will remain rampant with uneven information flow. Trying to be an outsider stock investor is like "being a drug-free athlete whose competitors are all juiced up on steroids." In the end, after all his experience, he has this to conclude:

> Individuals should not be buying individual stocks. I know this is a radical statement, especially coming from a guy who researched individual stocks for a living. But there are simply too many insiders with too many unfair advantages.[22]

The Case for Index Units Over Stock Picking

If picking stocks based on the fundamentals is not enough to protect capital, what other tools can we use?

At our firm, we decided to stop the game of picking individual public stocks years ago. Some people find stock picking a rewarding trade-off for the time invested; we, simply put, do not. In our view, no exterior analyst, no matter how gifted, can know a company from the inside vantage of its operations managers. As a way of fulfilling due diligence, analysts should talk to management personally. Many develop close working relationships of necessity. Most business leaders are charismatic, impressive people. This can be a threat to the constant objective assessment that valuable risk managers must practice. We cannot afford to fall in love with any company or its management. Our primary concern is with not losing chunks of our client's precious capital and with making them real gains during their lifetime.

As market capital flows away from stocks to safer havens at the end of a business cycle, we must not be torn or constrained by other agendas. There is no point in standing in the path of a stampeding crowd intent on leaving a building to tell them, "Wait, I disagree. I did the math on the data and the shares are worth their current price." This will get you flattened. We decided long ago to step aside, ego in check, and calmly wait for the dust to settle. Once it does, with capital still intact, we can go back in and pick up our investments at lower prices. To participate in equity markets in an impartial and nimble way, our equity tool of choice is not individual company shares but rather exchange traded funds and index units.

The primary factors dictating the performance of stock markets around the world are macro-economic elements: the business cycle, inflation, and interest rates. During the expansion—stage II to IV of the business cycle (see the business cycle chart in chapter 2)—stocks tend to rise in concert; in stages V, VI, and I, stocks tend to drop in concert. Within this broader context, during the economic expansion, different sectors will outperform at different times.

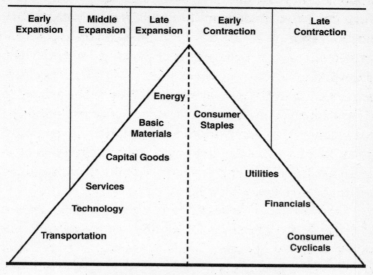

One Complete Economic Cycle

Source: John Murphy, Intermarket Analysis, (Wiley), 2004

When interest rates are falling and the economy is bottoming, financial stocks tend to be the best-performing sector. At this point in the cycle, it is most likely beneficial to hold the shares of high-quality financial companies. Timing entry and exit points in the individual sectors is, for us, more productive than forming an opinion, no matter how reasoned, as to which major bank is likely to outperform another over time. When bank shares are receiving large flows of capital because their earnings are rising, we wish to hold them. When they start to be sold in broad volume because their earnings are contracting at the end of an economic expansion, we wish to sell them.

Using index units for equity exposure, we are able to efficiently enter and exit particular sectors and countries without having to take on the risk of individual companies. We are able to remain impartial and focused on the big picture of the economic cycle rather than being consumed with the ambitious task of outsmarting the rest of the market with individual stock picks.

Chapter 7
The Media

*Trying to determine what is going on in the world
by reading newspapers is like trying to tell the time
by watching the second hand of a clock.*
—Ben Hecht

One of the big contributing factors to market hype and irrational price behaviour is the extent to which human beings can influence one another by their views. By the late '90s, the advent of business television and market watch shows were an incredible source of oxygen for the fires of market mania. The media serves to magnify and reinforce popular psyche.

There is virtually constant coverage of the markets and market movers around the world. Regular investors have access to endless amounts of information and commentary of people "in the know." In the '90s, this became big business in and of itself. There is no doubt that mass media of print, radio, and television are great consensus-building machines. More information is supposed to lead to more efficient markets (or so the theory goes), but the opposite frequently becomes the case. The more irrational investors become, the greater the inefficiency in their markets.

One of the shows that started around the market peak in 2000 was CNBC's *Kudlow & Cramer*. Every evening at 8 p.m., world viewers could tune in to very learned commentary from a sophisticated economist, Larry Kudlow, and a self-proclaimed "star hedge fund manager," Jim Cramer. The two hosted many friends and colleagues to debate financial issues on the show. These types of shows can provide interesting banter, so long as you do not expect them to be right in their predictions. All throughout the bear market of 2000–2002, these guys were supreme bulls. They argued learnedly that there was no good reason for world markets to decline much further as the underlying economy had never been better—the U.S., never stronger. They said they were buying stocks throughout, and yet, month after month, the markets sunk lower. How could people so bright and so in the know be of so little use to anyone trying to protect and grow their invested capital?

In late April 2006, I was in a hotel gym and happened to catch an episode of *Kudlow & Company* on the overhead television. By then, Jim Cramer had parted company with Kudlow and moved on to his own solo show called *Mad Money* on CNBC, where he literally rants and raves buy recommendations at his viewers. On the day I was watching, Kudlow had five esteemed guests, all whom he introduced as his buddies. He then went on to ask them if they were concerned that the incredible gains of the energy and commodities sectors may be presenting a cycle peak and a time for investors to take some profits. None of them thought the incredible gains presented any cause for concern. None suggested downsizing one's exposure as a reasonable course. They all said the economy could not be any better. Kudlow commented that it was amazing they were all in agreement with him and that things were only looking up. We shall see, I murmured under my breath. It was Galbraith who said, "In economics, the majority is almost always wrong." As a money manager, I am frequently reminded of what it must be like to grow up in a dysfunctional family where one of the members is a drug addict but the other members refuse to admit it. The family member who sees the problem and admits things are abnormal may be shunned as crazy.

When I first waded into financial analysis, I did so with a great hope that it would reveal some of the answers about why the investment world seemed as it did and what I could do better to make clients money. Listening to other company analysts, journalists, and executive officers had proven of no value in preserving and growing client capital. I had personally owned shares in WorldCom and Nortel and know the experience of real loss, but I had also owned shares in General Electric and bank shares. While considered the bluest of the blue chips, conservative companies still can drop about half their value in a down-cycle.

Few people who are hosted on business channels have any reason to forecast market declines, as Reingold puts it:

> ... investors need to be reminded that the various
> strands of advice they are receiving come from people
> who have their own potentially conflicted agendas.
> That could be anyone from television commentators
> to journalists, analysts, bankers, or other groups.[23]

Business leaders and CEOs are there to sell the story of their business. Mutual fund managers and company heads are paid to sell the long-term benefits of holding equities. Economists and analysts who work for major securities firms are there to sell people the firm's securities. Only independent analysts and portfolio managers are free to see the good and the bad when looking forward. Many of them are reluctant to speak out publicly if the markets appear poised for decline. They can manage the capital entrusted to them in accordance with their discipline and rules, but to speak out on national television is a risky proposition. If the market goes against them for a while after they do so, people may start to believe that the manager is inept.

Many value managers who stuck to their discipline in the late '90s sold most of their equities before the market peak. Some did so as early as 1997 when valuations could no longer be justified on a rational basis. Many moved to a large weight of cash as the madness raged on through 1998 and 1999. Many began to experience incredible redemption rates as clients decided the managers were wrong to be out and were costing them missed opportunities. Oblivious to the risk, clients wanted to run back into the burning building. At mania peaks, the mass consensus seeks to overwhelm con- trarian voices.

When we appear as guest managers on business channels, my partner and I are two of the independent few who are free to call it as we see it. We are constantly reminded of the na- ture of the beast as we partake in the revolving line of talking heads brought out for their brief sound bites.

Recently, I was waiting in a studio's green room with the CEO of a large income trust who was appearing to announce the firm's results. Mr. CEO paced the room, muttering com- plaints about his executive assistant's notes, as two support- ing thirtysomething MBAs carried his bags and jumped at his every request. Their PR lady arrived to calm him down and pump him up with some final words of encouragement. "We have the press conference at 10 a.m., so there will be plenty of time to make it to the hotel after this spot," she assured him. "Remember to look upbeat and tell the good news," she reminded him. "Yes, let's tell the good news and pump the sunshine. Let's sell this story!" the CEO exclaimed in a scrumlike huddle.

After the appearance, the team congratulated their fearless leader with great compliments and back patting about the job he had done onscreen. "Good luck and have fun on your appearance," he nodded towards me on his way out. "Thanks," I said, "it's always fun here in the belly of the beast." "Belly of the beast?" he gave me a confused look. "Belly of the beast?" he repeated as he walked out and onward to his next appearance.

When TV market coverage first arrived, famous market technician John Magel insisted on insulating himself from the daily news, reading only daily quotes and two-week-old copies of the *Wall Street Journal*. "We read the tape, not the tube," became his motto.[24]

The media and business channels exist to report current information with as much sizzle as possible. Many of the commentators are consummate professionals who do their job very well. However, the bulk of the content is provided by industry proponents in their mantra of buy, buy, buy. Despite its entertainment value, it can be perilous for investors to accept the information at face value. Media experts can be impressive and bear considerable psychological influence on us. We must filter this information and always be mindful of any inherent bias in a messenger.

Section III

The Myths

Chapter 8
About Risk

Only a fool tests the depth of the water with both feet.
—African proverb

Investing is a bet on an uncertain future. It necessarily involves hope for a future outcome. The less cash flow an investment pays while you wait, the more hope you need to have. At peaks of the stock market, prices have gone up relative to the dividends stocks pay and so the dividend yields are historically low. Over the past 200 years, U.S. stocks averaged dividend rates of over 4%. By 2006, the average yield on the S&P 500 companies had dropped to less than 2%, which was the second lowest dividend yield ever in the last 100 years. Dividend yields had been just over 1%, the lowest ever in history, at the market peak in 2000.

So less cash flow or dividend yield means you need more hope that the stock price will increase while you hold it. Investment risk is the probability of your hopes being dashed and your capital not adequately rewarding you for the risk you expose it to.

As the fathers of modern portfolio theory postulated their ideas in the early and mid-1900s, the focus of their analysis was really upon the calculation of expected returns. By the time the young Harry Markowitz stumbled into the arena in 1952, he was struck by how little attention was paid to the fallback plan. Markowitz pointed out that investors couldn't just focus on expected returns, because we have to worry about risk too. He defined risk as the likelihood that our actual returns may fall short of our expected returns over time. Markowitz has spent much of his career working on the most efficient way to combine assets in a portfolio for optimal return at a given level of risk.

In 1952, Markowitz wrote fourteen pages that shook the world. They were published in *The Journal of Finance* under the unassuming title "Portfolio Selection." Up until this time, most finance theory was focused on individual securities and their expected returns. Markowitz's work examined not just the hopes but also the risk or volatility capital endured in seeking returns. He wrote that the logical first step in determining optimal asset mix "starts with observation and experience and ends with beliefs about the future performance of available securities. The second stage starts with the relevant beliefs about the future performances and ends with the choice of portfolio."[25] In this sense, we must first examine where we are in a particular economic cycle and make educated assessments of what the expected returns are likely to be over the coming months on the various assets such as cash, bonds, and stocks. If we are facing an economic downturn, where stocks are likely to drop in value, one might wisely opt to reduce equity exposure. An investor is not likely to be rewarded for taking "dumb risk." If prospects for stocks are poor, bearing the risk of holding them is likely to be an inefficient trade-off between our risk and its negative reward. We should assess expected returns for various asset classes and weight a portfolio accordingly.

In an investment culture focused on equity sales,

Markowitz's work has been widely misquoted. The theory became contorted in the bull of the '80s and '90s where average returns were above the long-term norms and interim pullbacks were relatively short-lived. Consequently, static return numbers were plugged into an efficient market formula, where 12 to 13% was consistently expected for equity returns and risk was defined as short "interim" downturns. People confidently quoted "obvious" and "immovable" facts about stock market returns as if they had always been thus.

In the fervour of bull markets, popular psyche can become wildly optimistic. Risk becomes defined as the "risk" of being out of a market. Risk is missing out on big gains; it is no longer about losing capital. The hallmark of overly optimistic times—borrowing to lever up and get more capital to invest—becomes popular. Mutual funds, stocks, real estate, and exotic tulip bulbs become the passion of the nation as more and more new investors become attracted to the hopes of striking it rich. And some do strike it rich. At least for a little while—on paper.

It is a common pattern in human history to have wise contrarians denounced for being fools or too old. Warren Buffett, the veteran investor who has masterfully run Berkshire Hathaway for the past forty years, has been periodically denounced when he has warned against dangerous market trends. Other oracles over the years have reported receiving death threats and hate mail when they too have spoken out against the prevailing "wisdom" of a time. Party poopers, it turns out, are not very welcome.

When prices are irrationally high, managers that pay attention to value will often be unable to buy. They must patiently wait for the inevitable decline before they can go back in. During the final throes of a frenzied peak, the best value managers will appear to be standing still. In 1999, Berkshire Hathaway posted a miniscule gain of 0.5% when the S&P

500 roared up 21%. But one or even a couple of years does not define the end. There is a reason that Buffett's fund has averaged twice the returns of the S&P 500 over the past forty years. His discipline has withstood the test of time to the benefit of the followers who stuck with him as the following table of results will attest.

Berkshire's Corporate Performance vs. the S&P 500

Year	Annual Percentage Change in Per-Share in Book Value of Berkshire (1)	S&P 500 with Dividends Included (2)	Relative Results (1)-(2)
1965	23.8	10.0	13.8
1966	20.3	(11.7)	32.0
1967	11.0	30.9	(19.9)
1968	19.0	11.0	8.0
1969	16.2	(8.4)	24.6
1970	12.0	3.9	8.1
1971	16.4	14.6	1.8
1972	21.7	18.9	2.8
1973	4.7	(14.8)	19.5
1974	5.5	(26.4)	31.9
1975	21.9	37.2	(15.3)
1976	59.3	23.6	35.7
1977	31.9	(7.4)	39.3
1978	24.0	6.4	17.6
1979	35.7	18.2	17.5
1980	19.3	32.3	(13.0)
1981	31.4	(5.0)	36.4
1982	40.0	21.4	18.6
1983	32.3	22.4	9.9
1984	13.6	6.1	7.5
1985	48.2	31.6	16.6
1986	26.1	18.6	7.5
1987	19.5	5.1	14.4
1988	20.1	16.6	3.5
1989	44.4	31.7	12.7
1990	7.4	(3.1)	10.5
1991	39.6	30.5	9.1
1992	20.3	7.6	12.7
1993	14.3	10.1	4.2
1994	13.9	1.3	12.6
1995	43.1	37.6	5.5
1996	31.8	23.0	8.8
1997	34.1	33.4	0.7
1998	48.3	28.6	19.7
1999	0.5	21.0	(20.5)
2000	6.5	(9.1)	15.6
2001	(6.2)	(11.9)	5.7
2002	10.0	(22.1)	32.1
2003	21.0	28.7	(7.7)
2004	10.5	10.9	(0.4)
2005	6.4	4.9	1.5

Average Annual Gain 1965–2005

21.5	10.3	11.2

Overall Gain, 1964–2005

305,134	5,583	299,551

Note: Data are for calendar years with these exceptions: 1965 and 1966, year ended 9/30; 1967, 15 months ended 12/31.[26]

Source: Berkshire Hathaway Annual Report 2005

Note the anatomy of an average: from 1965 to 2005, Berkshire only reported a loss once, being -6.2% in 2001. The S&P itself suffered almost twice that loss in 2001 and recorded negative returns a total of ten times over the same time period—on average, the index lost value once every four years. Through strict attention to price and with preserving capital as the number one focus, Buffet and company have been able to more than double the returns of the overall market for forty years, *with much less volatility (risk)*. Investors can learn much about the anatomy of an average return by carefully studying such real-life results. In order to average 21.5% over this 40-year period, Berkshire shareholders didn't have to repeatedly suffer through losses, but they did have to suffer through years where the overall market went up more (and sometimes incredibly more) than their fund! In other words, in order to outperform substantially over time, the fund sometimes had to patiently underperform in roaring bull markets so that it was ready and waiting to take advantage of buying opportunities when market prices were driven down again in bear markets.

People have short and selective memories. During periods of great excess, many investors seem to only see prices going up. They don't know their risk tolerance until they have seen real risk up close. There are many painful outcomes when the reality of risk finally hits. There were so many prolific stocks in the bull of the late '90s. Global technology was expanding, and to the masses, there was no glimpse of a slowdown in sight. Perpetual economic expansion was considered the birthright of the new millennium.

One of the poster companies of this new era was Nortel Networks. The difficulty with Nortel was that it had no actual net income. It had many hopes and prospects for the future, but investors began paying for its future as if it were money in the bank and the share price skyrocketed to over $120 per share. This income-free wonder came to represent 34% of the Canadian stock market index. Perhaps most unfortunately, many of the people who came to own Nortel were widows and orphans who had previously held shares in its parent company, BCE (a phone company), and received the shares of Nortel as a distribution spin out. Old folks suddenly found themselves with a half a million dollars in one high-tech company share. But the popular love was so great that few people saw reasons to sell it. Why sell something that had made us all so suddenly rich? "Why trigger the gain and pay income tax?" was the common refrain.

One retired BCE executive I met held several million dollars of Nortel shares. In its price surge over a couple of years, the position had grown to represent about two thirds of the man's net worth. I told him it was an overexposure and he should downsize the risk to protect the capital. I forwarded some general comments on the merits of diversity and the tendency of assets like Nortel to drop to their long-term average price. Unfortunately, like many former employees of Enron, WorldCom, and others, he assured me that he felt comfortable holding the shares of his old employer. He was familiar with their business. Volatility, he felt, was not a concern. Shortly thereafter, the share price began its horrible plummet from $124.50 to $0.67. The millions of dollars became a smoking hole at the man's feet. Six years later, the shares had not yet recovered above $4. This is a common story, but obviously one of considerable pain.

I have heard the debate over whether diversification is a good thing or a wimpy thing many times. Those who argue it is for wimps usually point to the fact that many of the world's wealthiest people made their money by investing most of their time and money into one business that paid off in spades. I would like to respond to this argument. Yes, it is true that people such as Microsoft co-founder Bill Gates or

Wal-Mart founder Sam Walton became billionaires by holding most of their net worth in the company they each built, but there are a few points that need to be acknowledged about this. First of all, these billionaires are the poster children for concentrated risk because *they survived to tell the tale.* Far more people took such risks and went bust, but we do not hear much about the losers. The list of big-bet-folks-that-made-good exhibits great survivor bias. The difference between a winner and a loser in this metric is clearly how much financial success they achieve in the end.

There is a difference, I would suggest, between taking a concentrated bet on a business you build from scratch and work in every day versus a business in which you are a passive outside investor. The hands-on owner/operator has more control and awareness of the intricate workings of the business than any passive investor could ever have. In this sense, we all take concentrated risks in our own business or profession, but to do so in other ventures in which we are logistically detached can be a reckless risk. It is for this reason that intelligent diversification remains a wise strategy for capital preservation.

In his book *Capital Ideas*, Peter Bernstein tells a happy story from his experience as an investment counsellor in the '50s. He tells of a fortysomething couple who visited his office one morning in modest attire. They advised him that they had come to retain his services as an investment manager and handed him a statement of a surprisingly significant portfolio. In a quick review, Bernstein noted that the entire account was comprised of shares of just three companies. Shocked at what he saw, he asked them what they hoped he could do for them. The wife explained. A few years earlier, her husband had lost his job. Their total life savings at that point had been $15,000 and they considered doing one of two things: they could live off their savings and be broke in one year or they could take their life savings and wager it all in the stock market. They opted for the latter and selected three stocks that were widely popular in the big bull market underway at that time.

As luck would have it, the couple's timing was perfect and a couple of years later, their $15,000 had grown to a mind-boggling sum. But since the money had grown so much, the wife had become increasingly unsettled. While she was supportive of their gamble at the outset, now that their capital had grown so large, she was having trouble sleeping and was worrying about little else. She had finally convinced her husband that they needed to now seek out a professional manager who could manage the portfolio and make it last for the rest of their lives. Fortunately, they came to Bernstein before the crash that followed soon after.

In our own practice, I have seen only a few good endings to lucky stock picks. One that comes to mind is the story of some elderly clients who turned $20,000 borrowed on a line of credit into a $500,000 windfall within a few short months on a dot-com in the late '90s. Fortunately, the wife was nervous about making sure that they retained the paper gains and she came to see us about how best to do so. We told them that such unusual gains were not common and it was crucial that they sell the shares to maintain their windfall. We devised a plan to systematically sell off parts of the position as the prices continued to rally over the coming weeks. The husband resisted our advice and continued to voice an interest in holding onto the shares, but the wife prevailed in convincing him otherwise. Kicking and screaming to the end, the husband insisted that they hold on to the last 1000 shares, as he felt confident they would only go up. Shortly thereafter, the company went bankrupt in the tech burst that followed. The clients, now in their late '70s, continue to finance their retirement years with the proceeds from selling off at the top.

These are happy endings. Such stories can be inspiring

where wisdom and self-restraint were able to triumph over greed and ignorant hope.

In the '90s, early retirement offers packaged a great many teachers off into retirement, making way for a wave of younger teachers to take their jobs. Retiring teachers had the option of either collecting their indexed defined-benefit pension for the rest of their lives or withdrawing a lump sum commuted value. Unfortunately for many, the timing of this offer coincided with the then prevailing mania and greed-inspiring gains of the stock market. During this time, we met with many teachers who were seeking advice on how best to invest lump sum rollouts from their pensions. When we reviewed their options, it was clear that the pensions were very valuable assets.

At a time of great financial risk in overheated equity markets and low interest rates, the teachers' pension offered guaranteed indexed payments for life with a survivor benefit option for the life of one's surviving spouse. Typical pensions offered were starting at $45,000 per year. This income stream would require more than $1 million in Government of Canada bonds to provide the same level of income and security of capital to the retiree, and yet, many teachers questioned whether the pension was good enough. Many had been lured to the dark side by the mania of the time and were calculating expected returns of more than 10% per year if they elected the lump sum withdrawal and piled it all into the flavour du jour: U.S. Equities.

As money managers, we are paid to manage assets, but we universally counselled these teachers to leave their money in their pension plan and select the monthly income. Many of them happily took our advice. Sadly, many of them never met with us. Many teachers seeking the "good news," found others who sold them on the idea of withdrawing their guaranteed pension funds and throwing a lump sum into the stock market of the late '90s. The results have been devastating to say the least. Even six years later, broad markets have only just recovered to prior levels, while tech and telecom sectors are still down (in some cases by over 80%) from previous levels. Meanwhile, the trend of the ever-escalating U.S. dollar has now fully reversed, sucking the market gains of foreign investors down with it.

In our practice, when reviewing the statements of prospective clients, we take every opportunity to circle any securities they are holding that have dramatically dropped in value or gone unvalued in their accounts. "This is what risk looks like," I tell them. As Crestmont Research founder Ed Easterling so aptly states in *Understanding Market Cycles*, "Risk is not a knob!" It is not something you can set at a pre-scribed level for an expected output and walk away. Risk is by its very nature an unknown. Risk means you can watch large parts of your capital evaporate before your eyes. Companies can go bankrupt and take your capital to zero. Markets can drop 50% or more and stay there for prolonged periods of time—sometimes years, sometimes decades.

Financial consultants are trained to ask clients preliminary questions to survey their risk tolerance before recommending an asset allocation. The questions tend to go something like this: "If the market value of your investments dropped 10 to 20%, how would you react?" In my opinion, this is rather like asking someone, "If martians were to invade the earth, how would you react?" The true answer is that until we have lived through such an experience, we really cannot say how we would react. Many people talk like they have a high risk tolerance before they are actually confronted with real risk. Until we or our loved ones have lived through a major health scare or suffered a big financial setback or held a portfolio statement with our name on it that has lost 10 to 60% of its value, it is difficult to talk about how we would react. Real-life experience is what shapes our views and ideas as we go.

At a distance, few people can appreciate the true risk of the stock market. Wise market experts understand the nature of the beast because they lived it first hand. As Bernstein puts it:

> At the extremes, the market is not a random walk. At the extremes, the market is more likely to destroy fortunes than to create them. The stock market is a risky place.[27]

This is a sobering and important message. Successful people learn from the feedback loop of their experience and make future choices accordingly.

One school of financial planning states that the more money a person has, the higher their risk tolerance, since wealthy people can afford to lose money and not have it jeopardize their hearth and home. In reality, I have found the exact opposite of this. Wealthy people are often the most risk averse. They already have enough money to live well and are usually not looking for investments to make them "rich" because they are already are. Most wealthy people hate to lose money. Capital preservation is their primary goal. Patience and prudence are some of the best traits an investor can have. The wealthy can afford to be patient and wait for exceptional investment opportunities—"wealthy people will take risks only if the expected return is big; people with limited funds will accept huge risks even if the possible return is only slight."[28] Wise investors are happy to hold cash and earn modest interest while they wait for the next good opportunity.

It is a sad irony that smaller investors with the least ability to absorb losses tend to be the most accepting of risk. Many believe that if they are brave or aggressive enough, they will somehow be able to hit the investment ball out of the park. It often happens that he who can afford it the least ends up losing repeatedly, and the investment sales world feeds on this weakness. In my years of investment counselling, I have found this paradox to be the most painful of all to witness.

Risk is often not our friend, and we must develop tools to counter the probability that our hopes will not be rewarded. A good friend of mine calls this the need to "drown-proof" our best-laid plans. The investment sales industry is paid to sell us risk, so we must dance with them at arm's length.

Chapter 9
About Borrowed Money

A man in debt is so far a slave.
—Ralph Waldo Emerson

"Well, it's started," one experienced appraiser told me. "I have done four power of sale appraisals in the first two months of 2006. I had only seen one in the seven years before that. Other homeowners are telling us, 'You had better appraise this high or you will be back here doing a power of sale shortly.'"

Borrowed money magnifies risk. If a person is carrying a lot of debt, they have less freedom of choice. They are dependent upon maintaining sufficient cash flow to pay for their life and to service their debt payments or risk insolvency. This is rarely a good thing.

A self-made friend was telling me recently how much he had learned from his father about what not to do with money. His father had been a spender who had supported the family lifestyle through much debt and great pride. He tried to manage his financial affairs in secrecy and rebuffed questions or suggestions from those around him. Ultimately, the family lost their house to creditors. "I learned from my dad that debt was a curse," my friend said. "He never discussed money matters with any of us, and yet, through his mistakes, he taught me to avoid debt in my own life. I think that has been a great help to me.

"Years later, I was working at a multinational software company. When the company stock was going up, everyone was happy, but when we had a bad quarter, I remember the senior VP's scrambling to cover their margin calls. Some would beg the CFO for emergency loans from the company to cover their mortgage payments. These guys were making a million bucks a year, but their lifestyle was hugely expensive. They had all the toys and all the debt to go with it. I learned from watching them that borrowing to invest can be a bad thing too."

When I was a child, my family lived a very middle-class lifestyle. For my parents, living debt-free was a major goal. My dad was an Irish immigrant and a builder by trade. Starting from their first tiny bungalow, my parents always built our homes themselves. They never had a mortgage because they built only what they could afford and did not buy fancy furniture, appliances, or cars. When they had the money, they bought what they could pay for with cash. As time went on, they moved us up to larger and more-equipped debt-free homes, one house at a time. My dad always told me that he did not want to have a mortgage so that no bank could ever kick us out of our home.

My grandparents lived in Detroit during the Great Depression and the experience was a lifelong tonic against spendthrift habits. They learned to live without borrowed money, having the discipline and restraint to save and only purchase that which they could afford.

When I started university, I had to fund myself with student loans and part-time jobs. At the time, student loans were a much-needed source of funds and I was grateful that I could get them. But there was a bad side to student loans: they conditioned me to think that debt was a necessary part of my life. Student loans are interest-free and payment-free until the student is finished with their studies. In my case, that payment holiday went on for seven years. I worked hard throughout my education and lived very frugally: dorm rooms and very basic clothing, no car, no summers in Europe. I was the student working in the school pubs so that I could wake up Friday mornings with no hangover and a pocket full of tips. By the time I finished law school, I was $60,000 in debt for my education.

My articling year was the first time I was able to work full time for a complete year and that first year's salary was $23,000. The monthly debt payments on my student loans began. On top of this, I could no longer live in a student dorm or come to work in running shoes. A student lawyer had to look like a lawyer and that meant spending some money on clothes. I used a couple of the credit cards that had arrived in the mail unsolicited. Creditors know that young professionals tend to be a good credit risk. This seemed rather flattering at the time; it was nice to have a bank say they trusted you. The debt trap descended.

By the time I was called to the bar, my new husband and I had borrowed $15,000 from my dad for the down payment on our first home, a $97,000 townhouse. We owed another $4,000 on credit cards. Our mortgage rate was 10.5% and was considered relatively low, as rates had been much higher in the '80s. My first job as a lawyer and my husband's first job at a securities firm paid us each $36,000 per year. We had been without a car, but now we leased a Honda Civic. We were a couple of "dinks"—dual income, no kids—and the expectation was that we should now be grabbing the rightly deserved brass ring, except that by the time we made our monthly payments, we had no income left over. Things were very, very tight, and somehow it was suddenly not okay to admit we were broke. We had a professional image to uphold. The weight of our negative cash flow was heavy. It was a great strain on our young marriage and our creative energy. "You guys have too much debt," my dad advised me one day. "Thanks for the news flash," I thought.

It took my husband and me the next ten years of solid work to dig ourselves out of the hole we had started in. Luckily for us, our health, abilities, and good fortune enabled us to get ahead, but it was not a path that I would wish upon my children.

With the break of the stock market bubble in 2000 and then the shock of 9/11, the threat of global recession loomed large. Investor psychology came crashing down along with the World Trade Center buildings. Central bankers stepped up with their most effective tool and slashed interest rates to 50-year lows. In the U.S., the overnight lending rate from the Federal Reserve to the regional banks was cut from 5% to 1% and remained there for one full year before policy shifted to a gradually rising rate environment again. The aim was to stimulate consumption by encouraging spending rather than saving, and it worked very, very well. There is always a lag time between when rates are changed and when the effects of the policy show up in the economic numbers. By the end of 2005, people in many developed nations were entering into their second consecutive year of record spending and negative savings rates. They were spending more than they made at their employment and they were using incredibly free-flowing credit to fund their deficits. If the '60s were about free lovin', 2000 to 2007 was about free spendin'.

Free-flowing credit funded the material aspirations of the masses. Nowhere was this more evident than in real estate markets. With mortgage rates at 50-year lows, luxury suddenly became affordable. Lavish granite kitchens, ensuite bathrooms, triple car garages, and lots of square footage became standard fare for the middle class. This phenomenon could be seen all over the developed world. Great demand fuelled great price increases. Sustained low interest rates meant that people could continue to refinance their properties over and over again. They could afford to strip newfound equity from many properties and buy other properties. The gift kept on giving as development was sparked in recreational destinations and condominiums all around the world.

The Habit of Saving Little and Spending More

North American % Ratio of Savings to Personal Disposable Income

	Canada	United States
1980	17.4	10.0
1985	15.8	9.0
1990	13.0	7.0
1995	9.2	4.6
2000	4.7	2.3
2001	5.2	1.8
2002	3.5	2.4
2003	2.8	2.1
2004	2.6	2.0
2005	1.2	(0.4)
2006	1.5	(1.0)

Sources: Statistics Canada, National Income and Expenditure Accounts, cat#13-001, U.S. Bureau of Economic Analysis, Economic Indicators

As the party picked up steam, central bankers around the world began to slowly turn back the spigot. By 2006, the overnight lending rate in the U.S. had increased more than five-fold from the low of 1% to 5.25%. And still the party raged on. This has been a common pattern through history, especially in North America. Once consumers have developed a habit of free spending and buying their heart's desire, it is hard to go back. People became complacent about their lack of savings and record levels of debt. Interest-carrying costs sneak up on us. At the same time, the demand for goods spurred incredible increases in the price of basic commodities and energy. Life got a whole lot more expensive for people, and suddenly (or so it seemed), the real estate market was no longer cooperating. No longer could one refinance to capture that year's dramatic equity gains.

Historically, interest rates have moved in long-term 15- to 20-year cycles. From their peak in 1981, rates began a long descent that helped to fuel equity and bond market returns up to 2000. Each generation is marked by its own experience. The boomers who had mortgages and owed money in the early '80s became debt averse. They had lived the horrors of scrambling to keep up with escalating borrowing costs. My generation came to its borrowing career in the early '90s, just as rates were halfway into their long swan song. From 1981 to 1991, 5-year mortgage rates in Canada had dropped from 21.5% to 10%. By 2005, thanks to the rate cuts following 9/11, posted 5-year fixed mortgage rates went to an amazing low of 5.27% (see following mortgage rate chart). Unaware of how attractive and unusual these rates where, many people complacently opted to not lock in a term and let the rates float so that they could pay interest as low as 3%. Credit card companies that previously had been careful with their approvals became eager to extend credit. Unsolicited credit offers flooded consumers and encouraged them to spend. Why save, when you can afford your heart's desire now?

Average Residential Mortgage Lending Rate — 5 Years*

(Per cent)

Year	Jan	Feb	March	April	May	June	July	Aug	Sept.	Oct	Nov	Dec
1984	12.55	12.52	12.82	13.51	14.26	14.53	14.96	14.45	13.99	13.72	13.25	12.74
1985	12.44	12.57	13.43	12.77	12.38	11.89	11.75	11.77	11.85	11.96	11.75	11.61
1986	11.67	11.94	11.66	11.12	10.60	10.87	11.06	11.00	11.10	11.25	11.25	11.17
1987	10.85	10.46	10.20	10.39	11.04	11.26	11.26	11.49	11.72	11.97	11.49	11.56
1988	11.73	11.49	11.08	11.04	11.29	11.41	11.40	11.92	12.16	11.79	11.78	12.13
1989	12.24	12.23	12.41	12.72	12.29	11.93	11.85	11.76	11.75	11.75	11.75	11.95
1990	12.01	12.42	12.92	13.67	14.21	14.03	13.97	13.56	13.40	13.21	13.04	12.49
1991	12.13	11.58	11.45	11.27	11.23	11.24	11.31	11.47	11.38	10.84	10.14	9.84
1992	9.71	9.68	10.06	10.37	10.14	9.72	9.26	8.72	8.54	9.23	9.33	9.48
1993	9.47	9.44	8.97	8.89	8.88	8.86	8.68	8.58	8.57	8.55	7.84	7.71
1994	7.33	7.20	7.89	9.43	9.48	9.80	10.69	10.33	10.01	9.84	9.85	10.25
1995	10.60	10.48	9.93	9.66	8.98	8.67	8.54	8.94	8.95	8.75	8.66	8.46
1996	8.02	7.79	8.16	8.48	8.47	8.48	8.48	8.01	7.94	7.50	7.01	6.94
1997	7.14	7.12	7.06	7.56	7.46	7.22	6.98	7.00	6.96	6.73	6.69	6.90
1998	6.90	6.84	6.84	6.79	6.92	6.90	6.90	7.08	7.32	6.73	6.94	6.69
1999	6.72	6.79	7.03	6.71	6.99	7.35	7.42	7.80	7.67	7.90	8.13	8.13
2000	8.34	8.43	8.24	8.23	8.50	8.34	8.18	8.08	8.08	8.08	8.04	7.81
2001	7.58	7.52	7.19	7.22	7.38	7.47	7.46	7.39	7.03	6.74	6.51	6.64
2002	6.62	6.59	6.80	7.00	7.00	6.98	6.90	6.61	6.49	6.50	6.47	6.39
2003	6.26	6.29	6.33	6.44	6.10	5.62	5.71	5.87	5.97	5.83	6.02	6.00
2004	5.78	5.51	5.31	5.56	5.82	6.06	6.10	5.97	5.94	5.95	5.87	5.69
2005	5.60	5.59	5.60	5.67	5.55	5.31	5.26	5.32	5.30	5.39	5.56	5.60
2006	5.65	5.75	5.78	5.88	6.05	6.12	6.26	6.24	6.13	6.01	5.99	5.89

We became a continent of credit junkies. We had declining then negative savings rates in North America, precisely in line with the falling rate trend of the past fifteen years.

Household debt as a percentage of GDP

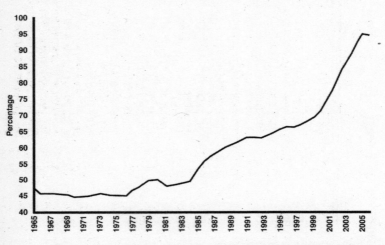

Source: Federal Reserve Z-1, Bureau of Economic Analysis

I have come to see credit and prescription drugs as some of the great ironies of our time. Prescription drugs afford us artificial health of sorts: we are able to abuse our bodies through poor diet and neglect and still live a long time, but the quality of life is often poor in the end, drugs notwithstanding. The same theme applies to widespread credit use; it may afford us artificial wealth for some time, but in the end, the quality of life and peace of mind tend to be diminished.

Home Mortgage Borrowing

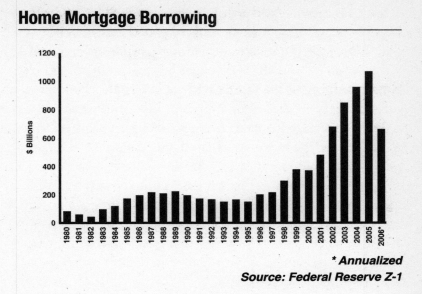

* Annualized
Source: Federal Reserve Z-1

The last time mortgage rates in Canada were as low as the early 2000s, was during the '50s. Low rates in the '50s led to the natural course of perilous overspending. The habit of the decade led to steadily higher interest rates over the '60s and '70s. Undaunted by the efforts of central bankers to contain it, inflation surged to a morbid peak in the early '80s. The baby-boomer demand for housing and consumables during this period has long been cited as the primary reason for the inflation that came to plague us.

Many have argued that current demographics do not support a recurrence of high interest rates since there simply is not the same concentration of borrowers in our aging population, and yet, household borrowings are at record levels. Higher debt appetite per person may have more than made up for the lack of population. Those borrowing to speculate on second and multiple properties escalated. Whether there is one person buying three properties or three people each buying one, demand cares not. While employment levels are high and interest rates relatively low, income is able to service monthly debt. But as a downside, risks surely are now higher. If the ability to sustain three properties depends upon the payments of one person, there is greater leverage and greater risk. Rising carrying costs, falling real wages, and soaring rental vacancy rates all prevail upon the speculator to place superfluous properties for sale. More sellers in a market drive prices down. The more prevalent the use of credit in the upcycle, the more magnified the downturn.

Credit offerings border on dark comedy at the peak of spending orgies. I received one email offering refinancing that perfectly captured the tenor of the times: "Your credit doesn't matter to us! If you own real estate and want immediate cash to spend any way you like…don't worry, your credit will not disqualify you!"

The U.S. government has been as unruly as its citizens during this period, funding escalating expenses through issuing many trillions of dollars in bonds to foreign investors while America continues to consume through imports much more than they export.

U.S. Trade Deficit

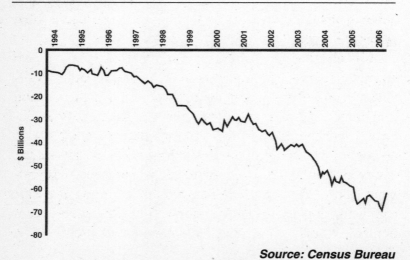

Source: Census Bureau

The net effect of all this debt will diminish our resilience to extraneous shocks that have always come and will do so again. Whether it be further terrorist events, an energy crisis, or a worldwide pandemic, debt-laden people and governments have a weakened ability to ride through crises.

"We are the undertakers," a trustee in bankruptcy said as he described his work to me. "We perform necessary duties but no one looks forward to needing our services. We are coming into our busy time now. It takes about a year from when rates go up to when people start filing for bankruptcy. People have been accumulating too much debt, they have been trying to keep swimming, but once rates have been rising for a while, a lot of them start drowning."

Borrowing to Invest

If borrowing to buy material things is usually a bad idea, what about borrowing to invest? It is common to borrow to buy your first home, and so long as you can work long enough to pay it off as quickly as possible, this strategy is often a successful way to get started. Borrowing to invest in the stock or bond markets is generally a less successful idea. Most people do not have sufficient tools or discipline to keep out of the markets when prices are high and get in again when prices are low.

It is characteristic of every mania that demand for cash prompts increased supply and credit becomes readily available. Credit affords people the buckets of gas to throw upon a smouldering fire. It is a sales strategy of the investment industry to encourage people to borrow to invest. People with no capital can be turned into worthy targets by gutting the equity in their homes or otherwise qualifying them for investment loans. "You are richer than you think," is one of the recent bank slogans prompting people to borrow against their homes. "Wouldn't it be nice if you could unlock some of the equity in your home?" "Live richer," is another. The only good mortgage, however, is one that is paid off. Unless we are interested in significantly downsizing to use our house equity, our home is our home; it is not a source of money to fund our lifestyle.

Using borrowed funds, a small client becomes a much larger income stream for their advisor. Many call this using other people's money—or OPM—to get rich. Opium comes to mind when I hear this. A drug pusher supplies his customers in the same way the investment sales industry promotes borrowing to buy its products.

One self-made millionaire I knew told me a story about margin that I shall never forget. In the late '70s, "John" was an entrepreneur and had his hand in a couple of different businesses. An Irish immigrant, he had worked hard to build up some equity. He had paid for his house, and he and his wife and four children were living a reasonable lifestyle. In the early '80s, the baby boomers had been borrowing up a storm to fund their demands for house and home. Inflation blossomed and central bankers responded with their standard tool: a barrage of interest hikes. Rates on Government of Canada bonds went well above historical averages. This was great for net savers and crippling for the masses that were borrowing to consume.

John felt confident that interest rates would have to turn down. He knew that when the rate trend finally broke and started down again, the price of existing bonds at current coupon rates would have to increase. He decided to bank on the upcoming change. He opened a margin account through his stockbroker and took out a line of credit against his home. He bought as many government bonds as he could. He started to use his margin account so that he could afford more bonds. At the time he started his plan, the 1-year Canada bond was paying an incredible 17%. Calling the top of a cycle is hard to do with complete precision. When you are using the magnification of leverage, calling cycle timing with precision becomes essential. Rates were due to drop, but it took another year before they did, and in the meantime, in 1981, prime lending rates went to 22.75%.

Thanks to John's borrowing, the negative leverage of rising rates and rising margin costs caused large drops in the value of his bond portfolio and it almost wiped him out. He called a family meeting and advised his wife and children that they were about to lose their house. His bet had gone the wrong way and all their savings had evaporated before his eyes. He spent many sleepless nights. Just as things looked beyond repair, the economy finally slowed, inflation began to subside, and the Federal Reserve and then the Bank of Canada started to cut rates. John's bonds began to rebound. The margin calls stopped. On the edge of personal disaster, John's equity began to crawl its way back.

When I first entered the money business, I remember seeing some federal bonds in client accounts at rates over 10%. At that time, rates had retraced to the 5% range and these "old" bonds seemed like surreal relics of a bygone time. Once rates began their long descent, it was hard to believe that they had once soared so high. To believe then that government rates could go below 3%, as they did in 2003, was unfathomable.

In every major market bubble, leverage becomes widely popular. "Leverage is your friend," is the rallying cry, and when investments only go up, leverage can be very good. But investments also go down, and unless you have an excellent sell discipline that will limit your losses, leverage can be financially fatal.

Long-Term Capital Management was the now infamous hedge fund that used leverage to soar and then crash from its start in March 1994 to its prolific demise in October 1998.

The founding partners were some of the most brilliant and respected academics and teachers in the finance field. Their plan from the outset was to set up an investment fund that would seek out arbitrage opportunities around the world by buying and selling bonds in different markets and capturing small profits in between. The way in which this low-return strategy became attractive was to use leverage to magnify tiny profits into big ones. The plan from the outset was to lever invested capital by at least twenty or thirty times. Up until April 1998, the plan went extremely well, but humans have a history of anomalous events, and 1998 was no exception. A bunch of seemingly unrelated world events reverberated through the U.S. Treasury market connected by a complicated, almost invisible, maze of derivatives.

Before the end of 1998, the trades had gone offside in epic proportions, evaporating in their wake some $4.5 billion of capital. It took the concerted effort of the world's largest investment firms to avert the bankruptcy of world capital markets. There was widespread outrage from investors. They had thought it their fair payment when gains were averaging more than 30% per year, but once results flipped over and the risk of the beast was revealed, most were shocked at their sudden misfortune. History is replete with examples of such "sudden" reversals of fortune, particularly where debt is employed. Roger Lowenstein's excellent book on the Long-Term Capital debacle makes this ageless point well:

> If you aren't in debt, you can't go broke and can't be made to sell, in which case "liquidity" is irrelevant. But a leveraged firm may be forced to sell, lest fast-accumulating losses put it out of business. Leverage always gives rise to this same brutal dynamic, and its dangers cannot be stressed too often.[29]

Leverage is a high-risk strategy for real-life people. Using it to magnify results increases the likelihood of financial ruin. Things must be priced to perfection in order for things to work favourably. Human experience is seldom perfect. To be financially successful, we need the greatest freedom and flexibility possible. Leverage can restrict our flexibility and debt threatens our independence and peace of mind.

An engineer friend of mine heads up a very successful commercial construction firm. Over lunch, we were discussing the business cycle and how a slowing economy would inevitably lead to some slowing in her company's revenue. "The thing is, we have no debt," my friend explained. "I can't tell you how many times accountants or business consultants will review our statements and tell us we should take on some more debt to increase our return on asset ratios. But you know, having no debt is one of the reasons we have survived and thrived for so long. It gives us flexibility. I don't have to underprice a job just to get the contract and pay the creditors. We can afford to be less desperate, more selective in picking the really profitable jobs. That keeps us out of big trouble. It keeps us able to sleep at night."

I often liken leverage to an addictive drug. Although it may feel good in the moment, it is often dangerous to our long-term peace and health. Some people will tell you that crack cocaine is the most incredible high ever. Okay, I say, let's concede that it is. Where does that take us?

Chapter 10
About Income

I'm living so far beyond my income that we may almost be said to be living apart.
—e. e. cummings

In the old days, workers typically had to fund their lifestyles out of the money they had left in hand from their earnings. This was what is meant to live within one's means. In recent years, however, such a modest approach has been rejected as boring and unenlightened. The conventional wisdom now insists we can spend our way to prosperity. This trend has been particularly encouraged since the accountability of debtor's prison was long ago replaced by the forgiveness of declaring personal bankruptcy. In modern times, it seems the repayment of one's debts is no longer considered an imperative of moral character. In *Empire of Debt: The Rise of an Epic Financial Crisis*, Bill Bonner aptly explains this phenomenon of our generation this way:

> People are determined to live large and live better than they can afford. They do this by what economists

136 — Juggling Dynamite

call smoothing income. Anticipating higher incomes in the future, young families spend the money now (e.g. buying bigger houses than they can afford). Nationwide, house sizes have grown 30 percent since 1980, says Cornell economist Robert Frank. And now even people in their '50s and '60s look forward to either higher incomes or miracles.[30]

In the habit of unfettered spending, many people also have unreasonable expectations about how much income their investment accounts can reasonably produce throughout retirement. This is often based on ignorance. Sometimes their expectations are misled by marketing material their financial advisors may use to attract clients.

The only "guaranteed" rates are high-quality government bonds and GICs. All investments are priced off of what we call the yield curve. This yield curve is the sum total vote of the bond market participants as to where interest rates are likely to go next. It sets the market price for bonds at all the different terms from cash to thirty years.

Led by baby-boomer and government spending in the '60s and '70s, interest rates levels soared, topping out in September 1981 with 5-year Government of Canada bonds yielding 18.78% (see following chart of bond yields). Anyone who had the ability and the foresight to buy a whole bunch of these bonds at those rates made a killing over the following years as rates began their inevitable trailing-off period and trending down all the way to a 3.2% in June 2005. These incredible rates were a guaranteed return on highly secure deposits, and yet, countless investors did not lock in these rates. In 1981, succumbing to classic human greed, many savers hoped and expected that rates might still go higher.

Selected Government of Canada Benchmark Bond Yields — 5 Years*

(Per cent)

Year	Jan	Feb	March	April	May	June	July	Aug	Sept	Oct	Nov	Dec
1980												12.53
1981	13.06	13.56	13.95	15.41	15.45	15.65	17.96	17.63	18.78	17.15	13.08	15.24
1982	16.17	15.00	15.21	15.08	14.88	15.98	15.83	13.79	13.08	12.30	13.52	10.42
1983	10.72	10.48	10.41	10.26	10.32	10.66	10.95	11.44	10.80	10.76	11.60	10.98
1984	11.02	11.53	12.14	12.52	13.39	13.42	13.24	12.68	12.40	11.81	10.81	10.90
1985	10.62	11.66	11.58	10.99	10.45	10.41	10.44	10.21	10.39	9.95	11.28	9.20
1986	9.80	9.49	8.97	8.56	8.95	8.80	8.88	8.80	9.04	9.01	9.52	8.63
1987	8.06	8.08	7.73	9.18	9.26	9.04	9.70	9.91	10.75	9.62	8.72	9.78
1988	9.02	8.77	9.14	9.41	9.49	9.50	9.75	10.23	9.97	9.61	9.88	10.27
1989	10.10	10.70	10.82	10.24	9.78	9.42	9.35	9.59	9.92	9.56	9.98	9.77
1990	10.02	11.09	11.29	12.23	11.39	11.09	11.04	10.63	11.25	10.88	10.07	10.27
1991	9.93	9.46	9.40	9.42	9.36	9.73	9.66	9.41	8.97	8.19	10.43	7.87
1992	7.93	7.97	8.52	8.49	7.91	7.45	6.53	6.53	7.35	6.76	8.16	7.34
1993	7.39	6.92	6.88	6.97	6.86	6.68	6.45	6.18	6.36	5.97	7.37	5.73
1994	5.40	6.12	7.47	7.44	8.01	8.82	8.96	8.32	8.36	8.55	6.01	8.99
1995	9.18	8.46	8.23	7.93	7.41	7.33	7.79	7.58	7.54	7.54	8.81	6.64
1996	6.33	6.87	7.02	7.09	7.01	7.05	6.96	6.60	6.28	5.59	6.74	5.44
1997	5.67	5.44	5.75	5.92	5.86	5.32	5.18	5.36	5.17	4.99	5.10	5.34
1998	5.09	5.26	5.11	5.32	5.21	5.28	5.42	5.62	4.78	4.69	5.17	4.76
1999	4.76	5.22	4.95	4.98	5.34	5.35	5.53	5.51	5.67	6.20	5.03	6.11
2000	6.38	6.29	6.13	6.17	6.17	6.04	6.00	5.92	5.76	5.75	5.98	5.30
2001	5.14	5.09	5.03	5.23	5.61	5.39	5.36	4.93	4.62	4.08	5.59	4.69
2002	4.71	4.58	5.28	5.05	4.90	4.67	4.30	4.49	4.20	4.34	4.68	4.06
2003	4.27	4.18	4.47	4.18	3.72	3.55	3.76	3.97	3.86	4.07	4.39	3.91
2004	3.71	3.47	3.35	3.81	3.96	4.07	4.07	3.83	4.00	3.94	4.07	3.74
2005	3.52	3.63	3.83	3.54	3.44	3.20	3.37	3.35	3.58	3.86	3.85	3.87
2006	3.98	4.02	4.13	4.38	4.31	4.53	4.25	4.03	3.88	4.08	3.85	3.95

Income investors have had a sobering ride over the past few years. Those who had higher-rate bonds from the earlier era fared well in that they were continuing to collect the high-interest payments from their bonds. But when reinvesting their money, they were facing lower and lower rates until finally it seemed that there was no point in buying bonds at all. The 10-year U.S. Treasury yield dropped to 3.4% and stayed there all the way to July 2005. Income investors were dying for yield. Even by 2006, with sixteen consecutive interest rate hikes by the U.S. Federal Reserve, the 10-year yield for the highest quality bonds one could buy sat at 5%. Over this same time frame, other alternatives became very popular, but not without the investor taking on a good deal more risk for the extra yield.

Understandably, income trusts became the rage as a surrogate for fixed-income investments during the declining rate years. Income and royalty trusts are equities with much less security than preferred shares and government bonds. The units are designed to flow cash from operations to the unitholders. This is how the trust pays out monthly or quarterly distributions and many of the "yields" are attractive at rates above 8%. But since the distributions are purely at the discretion of management and dependent on the success of the underlying business, they are in no sense guaranteed. If a company becomes insolvent, trust unitholders are last in line for payment of their principle and only out of any assets left-over after creditors, bondholders, and then preferred share-holders are paid. Much like the investors who received Nortel for holding BCE shares, many income trust investors had not yet seen the risk inherent in their favourite holdings.

On October 31, 2006, the Canadian government announced an upcoming change to the previously enjoyed tax breaks that had made income trusts so popular with investors. The trust market index plunged more than 18%, with many individual trusts losing significantly more. Many retired people who had loaded up on trusts for the high payouts were hurt. Many were angry with the government for their losses. Most of these people had no business holding so much of their retirement nest egg in this high-risk asset class in the first place. Reaching for higher income, many investors unwittingly place too many of their hard-saved dollars in the higher risk plays. Unfortunately, this is a common pitfall.

Retirement years should focus first and foremost on capital preservation and only second on the tax efficient income that it provides. But the low-rate environment served to turn these objectives around. Instead, investors focused on the highest tax efficient income first and at all cost. Capital preservation goals became secondary. This is a serious problem where retired people are living a lifestyle that is dependent on the continued distributions from the trusts. The financial sales industry is always happy to sell people equity-based investments and they have run long with the pitch on these products. I am reminded of past peaks in other markets where the uptrend had been so strong for so long that people became complacent about risk to capital. The focus shifts to "get me in before I miss out."

Financial sales advisors promising more than going bond rates often use equities as an income product for clients. A common strategy is to set up automatic monthly withdrawal plans from client accounts to pay them income, but this income withdrawal rate is not set based on the interest or dividend income earned in the account. It may be based on a little bit of actual income in the account, but the bulk is based on the expectation of capital gains growth. So withdrawal rates are routinely set at 8 to 10% per year. People are oblivious to the risk to their capital because they want to believe that withdrawing cash at these elevated levels is a sustainable plan. Many advisors believe it too.

When the party music ends, investors and many of their sales advisors are caught off guard. Collecting account withdrawals of 8% is no consolation when the market value of your investments drops 50% in a market downturn. Everyone becomes shaken by losses to capital. The clients blame the advisors. The advisors blame the clients in addition to the analysts that had been issuing all the buy recommendations. The analysts blame the terrorists and other geo-political shocks.

Actually, it is everyone's fault. Investors often buy wholeheartedly into good news because that is what they want to hear. The only plan that makes good sense is to structure your affairs in a long-term sustainable plan. This means the primary focus has to be on capital preservation. This also means that we cannot base our income withdrawal plan on hope, but rather we must structure our affairs to live off of the actual interest and dividends in our portfolio and only withdraw what that provides. In our current environment, we can withdraw no more than 4% per year without a high probability of eroding capital as we go.

I have met many people in the past few years who suffered painful losses in the market collapse of 2000 to 2002 without having accepted the lesson. They are still hoping that someone out there can safely get them 8% per year. When I tell them that they cannot currently withdraw more than 4% per year safely, many will tell me that another advisor assured them they can take 8 to 10% per year. I point out that the 8 to 10% is not a GIC rate and it is not a real promise but rather a sales pitch based on hope. Currently, risk-free rates on government bonds are at 4% and the dividend yield on the average S&P 500 company is less than 2%. When an advisor quotes a return hope of 8 to 10% on a balanced portfolio, they are pricing into the equation about 2% of cash in hand from dividends and 6 to 8% of hope for capital growth. Hope for long-term capital growth at average rates of 5 to 8% in developed markets is a pipe dream. When I tell people this, many shake their heads in disbelief. Some thank me for my time and go back up the street to the broker or mutual fund salesperson who said they could get them the 8 to 10%.

Some time ago, a woman contacted us after finding our web address through a newspaper article written about our focus on capital preservation. "Mary" told us how her partner had been seriously injured in a car accident and was soon expecting a million-dollar settlement from the insurance company. She was trying to do some research because it was her job as caregiver to look after the money and her spouse. They had no children and they did not own a house but were planning on buying one.

Over the course of probably ten emails over the next few weeks, we learned Mary's story and were quite moved. I informed her that $1 million would not produce a great deal of after-tax income safely and that they needed to be very careful with how they invested it.

I asked about the house she wanted to buy and determined that it would require perhaps $300,000 or $400,000 to buy a decent place in their area that would suit their needs. I suggested setting aside $400,000 in a savings account for a house fund and that she should start looking carefully. I told her how real estate was often overpriced in current markets and that she should be very careful about price so as not to overpay. On the remaining $600,000, I recommended a very-low-risk income-orientated strategy since neither of them was now able to work. A low-risk portfolio meant she should hope to earn no more than 6% per year, as the funds had to last for the rest of their lives. At forty-five, this could be a very long time. I also suggested that she should be sure to get a joint annuity quote as well as a structured settlement quote so that she could compare all of the low-risk options to find the one that best suited their needs.

A few months later, she emailed me again saying they were now ready to proceed and she asked me to send her a proposal for the way we would structure the account. I sent a basic outline suggesting that their $600,000 should be at least 65% high-quality fixed-income investments and that the remaining 35% could be in equities, but they too needed to be carefully managed to control the risk of loss. She should plan to withdraw no more than 4%, or $24,000, per year so that their withdrawals don't erode the capital. Also, the fees she will pay for management should be kept below 1.25%, as low fees are directly related to the success of the plan.

A few weeks later, I heard from Mary once again. "We have reviewed all the options presented as you suggested. I am sorry to advise you that we have decided to go with a financial planner whom my mother knows. She has done us a portfolio of mutual funds that will get us 8% per year, and that is twice as much as you have offered. I appreciate all the time and advice that you have given us, but I must say I was a little disappointed to see that you were offering us so little."

I will make a sad prediction: Mary and her spouse will not make 8% in income per year. They may have a honeymoon period where they will start to collect monthly withdrawals from the account, and they will be very happy with the intelligence of the advisor who has set them up with this wonderful plan. After the first year or so, possibly sooner, depending on the market cycle, they will notice that their account value is dropping each month and they will ask their advisor why. The advisor will assure them that the drops are just short-term fluctuations and that over time this will all even out. It won't, and within a couple of years, especially when the next market correction starts, Mary will start to panic at how quickly their capital is becoming eroded. She will start to doubt her advisor, will want different investments, and will want to hear someone else's good news. More than likely she will find herself stuck in back-end loaded mutual funds that she cannot escape from without paying a further 4 or 5% in exit fees. Beaten and tattered and missing a large chunk of the portfolio, Mary will leave her advisor for someone else, likely to repeat the same cycle over again.

The wish must never be allowed to father the thought. The hope for a high level of income must never be allowed to structure the portfolio. We have to properly structure our account first and then structure our affairs to live off the income that the investments safely provide. We need to live off our income when we are working; we must do the same when we are investing. This often means spending less and saving more and perhaps downsizing our material acquisitions. For some retirees, this will mean renting out their basement, downsizing their home, and/or maintaining an income from part-time work. This is the truth and it is the only answer that will serve us well over time. Pipe dreams are very painful and expensive things to maintain.

Section IV

The Keys

Chapter 11
Timing Markets

The intelligent investor is a realist who
sells to optimists and buys from pessimists.
—Benjamin Graham

You may have heard the popular saying, "A good time to buy stocks is whenever you have the money." Good for whom? one should ask.

When big banks, insurance companies, and mutual funds began combining and amalgamating more and more in the '80s, the push for normalized earnings became stronger. Normalizing earnings means keeping management fees rolling in, and this requires unitholders to stay invested. "Stay the course," "Look at the long term." The public became flooded with a barrage of carefully quoted facts that supported this industry view. One of the most manipulated and misused of such slogans was the oft-quoted phrase, "It's time in the market, not timing the market."

One widely used marketing piece cites the dismal investor returns obtained should one miss the nine best days in the market. And so, the logic flows, one can never afford to be out of the market for fear of missing out on some of the upside. What the sales industry does not acknowledge is what investor returns would be where one missed out on some of the worst days in the market. Crestmont Research publishes these numbers on their web site.

Profile of Best and Worst Days in the S&P 500

Examples from 2002 & 2003	2002	2003	Combined
Percent of Days Up	44.2%	54.8%	49.5%
Annual Return (S&P 500 Index)	(24.2)%	26.4%	(2.1)%
Worst 10 Days (Total Return)	(28.4)%	(20.5)%	(24.6)%
Return Without Worst 10 Days	5.9%	59.0%	29.8%

Source: Crestmont Research, www.crestmontresearch.com

In fact, history shows that investors who avoid the big market downturns need only capture 30% of the next upmarket cycle in order to fare just as well as perpetually invested and therefore more risk-exposed buy-and-hold investors.[31]

Numbers such as these make it very difficult to argue that there would not be lasting benefits were investors able to step out of markets and avoid the bulk of ugly price corrections and the resulting losses. As economist and author Ben Stein notes:

> Wall Street has been saying: You cannot time the market; buy stocks today, regardless of price, since stocks always go up in the long run. Our findings are exactly the opposite, and yet they agree perfectly with everyday experience. Far from being an irrelevant factor that we should dismiss from our minds when purchasing stocks, price appears to be an extraordinarily important factor that we ignore at our peril.[32]

Over thirty years of market experience have shown Stein this important truth that all long-term market experts know: timing is key. Sadly, it is too often the regular people who are purposely kept out of the loop, as assets are sold from strong hands to weak.

Some years ago, a journalist wrote to us that a prospective client of ours had asked for her opinion about our management style and that she had ventured to our web site to have a look. "I told the person I had never heard of your firm, but that you must be higher risk because you use indexing and market timing," she wrote us. In this automatic assumption that added risk is linked with an active strategy, the journalist was not alone. It is a widely held belief that if you are choosing times to enter and exit markets, you must be increasing portfolio risk. At least in our case, her assumption was without foundation and her comments reminded us of the enormous counter-education that needs to be done.

Let me be clear, I am not here advocating a day-trading strategy in and out of stocks. I have neither expertise nor interest in day trading. What I refer to as market timing is the buying and selling of equity holdings within the broader context of the roughly 4- to 5-year business cycle.

There seems to be vehemence on the part of many mainstream financial commentators to refute the notion that anyone can use market timing to the investor's greater benefit. I have tried to understand why this might be and confess I have no clear explanation. I suspect it is because the mega marketing dollars of the mutual fund industry have been successful. People have been programmed to believe that passive holding is investing and that any effort at timing is speculative. Who can honestly argue that there would be no benefit in buying the technology index in November 1998 and then selling it again in March of 2000? Or what about buying real estate before the many boom times in history and then selling it again before bubble-like prices revert to their long-term mean?

Why are so many people apparently threatened by anyone who can benefit from the ongoing swings in overall markets? Perhaps it is because it takes discipline—and true discipline, like strenuous physical exercise, cannot be faked. To reap the benefits, one must maintain good habits with patience consistently over time. Many may think of it, but few ever develop their own rules for doing so effectively. Many have tried and many have failed, but several others have succeeded. Why is this so hard to accept? We understand that it is wise to buy many consumer goods in their off-season when they are discounted, why not investments?

In the revised edition of Benjamin Graham's book *The Intelligent Investor*, editor Jason Zweig refers to a "leading financial planning" newsletter that had canvassed dozens of advisors as to how prospects should go about selecting an advisor. A few of the suggested questions include:

> What is your investing philosophy? Do you use stocks or mutual funds? Do you use technical analysis? Do you use market timing? (A "yes" to either of the last two questions is a "no" signal to you.)[33]

Here, he suggests that anyone who even mentions the terms "market timing" or "technical analysis" should be summarily rejected. This is notwithstanding the fact that any truly independent manager worth their fee will actively manage portfolios for entry and exit points that offer an advantage. The vast majority of managers are fundamental analysts of one kind or another, but many also use some form of technical analysis to help assess market risk and price history.

In the spring of 2004, I attended a money managers' conference. One of the speakers was a VP for the Canada Pension Plan (CPP) Investment Board. He held a doctorate and a

CFA. One of his more memorable comments was that "active management was a zero-sum game." For a moment, I had flashbacks of Jeremy Siegel and his confident assertions that being fully invested in stocks was all one ever needed. Evidently, the VP either did not care or notice that his audience was a few hundred money managers who spend all their working hours attempting to add enhanced gains and reduced risk to the portfolios under management. His comments underlined that he was speaking from the comfort and confines of a perfect theoretical bubble. The CPP, he went on to explain, was a $200 billion fund with an infinite time frame, which, thanks to projected contributions from current workers, had no need to generate any cash distributions for the next seventeen years, with very modest rates of withdrawal after that.

It is a serious error for such management assumptions to be applied to the portfolios of regular folks with finite lifespans. Let us clearly distinguish between theory and reality. Modern Portfolio Theory looks at long time spans (e.g. fifty years) and concludes that over the long term, an efficient portfolio of stocks and bonds can be passively held to one's benefit. What it does not address is the fact that individuals have many life events and psychological foibles that make this time frame ridiculously long. Furthermore, it fails to acknowledge that there have been many periods in history when passively holding stocks over 5-, 10- and 20-year periods would result in real sum losses to investors.

The bear market from April 2000 through to October 10, 2002 was the most severe since the Great Depression. Though severe, this type of environment is common throughout market history, and when prices are high in any market, so is risk to capital. There have been many bad times to buy stocks and bonds, and many times when it would have been much better to liquidate these holdings. But in order to strategically reduce exposure to an asset class, a manager must have the discipline of pre-set sell rules and the freedom to implement them.

Many managers do not have objective sell rules in place. Their rules are often based on subjective inputs that can be readjusted as time goes on in keeping with the general market temper. Since the general market temper is often widely held yet completely wrong, this presents the risk that individual managers might lack the objectivity required to make realistic risk assessments as they go. Other times, these decisions are restricted by firm policies born of politics and underwriting considerations. It could also be the fact that management fees can fall when moving to money markets. Also, funds sometimes hold such a large position of a stock that selling it would move the market price adversely against them. And then there is the "over the long term" argument that insists things will all work out without sweating the interim market movements—many "fundamentalists" stick to this approach.

The following chart shows the remarkable correlation between mutual fund managers and a passive market index in down markets.

What Protection in a Down Market?

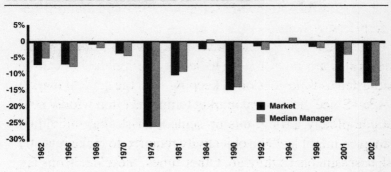

Source: The New Investment Frontier III

Evidence like this is often used to support the thesis that there is no benefit in paying an active manager when down-market losses are exactly the same as passively holding an index. There is no virtue, then, in active management, or so this argument concludes. However, what this study actually shows us is something quite different: it unequivocally proves that the vast majority of mutual fund managers are not truly "active managers." They are "equity managers." To be a true "active manager," a portfolio manager must be free to make strategic tactical asset selection across all of the major asset classes, which include equities, bonds, currencies, commodities, and *cash*. An "equity manager" in the mutual fund business will always buy just that—equities.

Active Equity Managers vs. Active Risk Managers

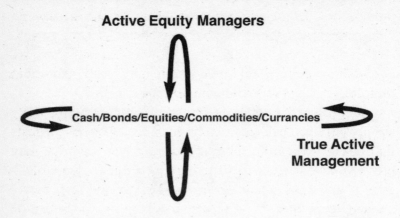

Active Equity Managers

Cash/Bonds/Equities/Commodities/Currancies

**True Active
Management**

In such a system, this bias persists even where equities
are not a good risk/reward trade-off for the investor and
where equities as an asset class experience large drops in
value within the context of each business cycle. It is for this
reason that mutual fund and other constantly long strategies
are not truly devised in the investor's best interests. Companies put their own interests of sustaining equity management
fees ahead of their fiduciary obligation to protect client capital first.

To justify their perpetually long approach, fund companies selectively quote the precepts of Modern Portfolio Theory, but the theory measures risk in very different ways than
regular folks do. It looks at various mathematical values such
as variance and standard deviation. These assess the fluctuations in market value of assets on either side of an expected
or mean return. Over long periods of time, these numbers
seek to quantify how much risk, or variability of returns, a
person has had to endure in order to make the return
"earned" over the same time frame. The difficulty is that
these concepts assume an infinite holding period. In other

words, they assume the investor will not buy at peaks or sell on any of the dips, but patiently hold through them. In these models, no one hits retirement and needs to take income, no one suddenly loses their job or their marriage, no one gets ill, and no one loses faith or reacts out of fear, and markets are assumed to move in relatively predictable patterns around their long-term compound annual return rates.

According to Benjamin Graham, equities aren't risky simply because they fluctuate in market value. He suggests that risk is present "if there is a danger that the price may prove to have been clearly too high by intrinsic standards— even if any subsequent severe market decline may be recouped years later."[34] To blindly invest at any price can be the greatest risk to an investor's long-term prospects. It may take many years for the stock to return to its previously elevated price. In addition, it is a great test of human nature to patiently hold an investment that has lost a great deal of its value in the hopes that it will recoup one day down the road. Years lost waiting to recover an initial investment is a significant loss for a single lifetime.

In general terms, we can think of the Andex chart as a long-term tribute to the constant struggle of human beings to push for improvement in their standard of living. Like a colony of working ants, we are all working hard year after year. Together we suffer from a herd mentality. Opportunity can be had by anyone who can break away from the group before its irrational exuberance takes it like lemmings over the cliff to the rocks below. How much harder or more improbable the climb is for anyone who must or chooses to liquidate out of panic at the bottom of the precipice. How painful it is for those who jumped in at the highest point in the market because that is where they joined the pack. How long does one spend devastated and driven away from stocks when risk is at its least and prices their lowest? These are the real-world factors that must be considered when deciding whether to attempt an effort at measuring price and market timing. In my real-life experiences, as a money manager for real-life folks, active management skilfully executed is far from a zero-sum game.

Theoretically, people could fare well by passively investing money in a broad stock index in their economy and not looking at it for thirty to fifty years, but this is just not what people do. This is because people are not pension funds: they do not have huge monthly savings or inflows to their investment account consistently throughout fifty years. They tend to make deposits and withdrawals in a lumpy fashion as they receive or spend cash flows. Generally, they look at their investment statements fairly regularly, and how patient or content they feel will most often be influenced by how other things in their life are going. People are influenced by the climate and the masses around them and they tend to be emotional and prone to weakness. They can make sporadic half-reasoned decisions. Investors do not react well to large market declines—most jump out at the bottom and want to invest more capital at the top. This is the reason the Dalbar study finds individual mutual fund holders greatly underperform historical return numbers of the indices and the funds themselves. So it is simply not good enough to say that markets are volatile and people should ignore this. Statistics show that people do not.

One of the most defining moments of a bull market can be found in the statements of participants that "this time is different" and the items in question have reached a permanent new price plateau, whether it be real estate, tech, or oil stocks. Good examples of timing issues in investing can be found throughout history. The history of gold makes this point repeatedly. Despite centuries of volatile cycles in this commodity, governments (who are just groups of people) have traditionally done as poorly as individual investors, opting to buy high and sell low. Gold was in a bear market for twenty years from 1982 to 2000, while stock and bond markets soared. It was during these down-cycles, where the commodity was the least in demand, that governments typically decided to downsize their holdings in reserve, selling large stores to the world markets at multi-year lows. The peak of the previous bull market in gold had been 1980, when the price per ounce increased from $64 in 1972 to $100 in 1973, then to $500 in 1979 to a peak of $850 in January of 1980. Remarkably, at the peak of the fear-filled price run in 1980, the U.S. government determined that it was best to continue to hold its vast gold reserves. It was not until the prices drifted down toward $350 and then below that central bankers opted to downsize their troves.

In his book *Where Are the Customers' Yachts?*, Fred Schewd, Jr. succinctly sums up the importance for individuals to time markets:

> When there is a stock-market boom, and everyone is scrambling for common stocks, take all your common stocks and sell them. Take the proceeds and buy conservative bonds. No doubt the stocks you sold will go higher. Pay no attention to this—just wait for the depression which will come sooner or later. When this depression—or panic—becomes a national catastrophe, sell out the bonds (perhaps at a loss) and buy back the stocks. No doubt the stocks will go still lower. Again pay no attention. Wait for the next boom. Continue to repeat this operation as long as you live, and you'll have the pleasure of dying rich.[35]

Chapter 12
Pursuing the Brass Ring

Wisdom outweighs any wealth.
—Sophocles

In the 1800s in America, a competitive element was added to the otherwise placid pursuit of riding a fairground carousel. Riders on the outside row of horses were offered the challenge of reaching for a single brass ring that was dangled from a metal arm that swung out once the ride had started. A rider who was successful in grabbing the ring could later redeem it for a free ride.

"Brass ring" came to denote a prize that one could reach for but was difficult to attain. "Grabbing the brass ring," "Going for the brass ring," or "Reaching for the brass ring" all became part of common parlance when referring to the opportunity to compete for a coveted prize. According to the American dream, reaching for the brass ring is synonymous with reaching for status and material success.

When I was a child, I used to tell people that when I grew up I was going to be a teacher, an actress, a dancer, a singer, a lawyer, and a writer. People would nod politely and say that I was very ambitious indeed. I spent my childhood doing most of these activities every day. I was creative all day long; I was very inspired. I even held summer Bible classes in my backyard for local kids in order to get a shot at teaching. Amazingly, groups of kids would show up to be my students. My parents found it humorous, but as I grew older, people around me would suggest that I had to be realistic and it was probably best to pick one "serious" career and focus on that. Saying one wanted to be creative was just too obscure, so I chose at first to be a writer and a teacher, and began an under-graduate degree in English literature.

I surveyed many of my professors during my undergraduate studies and most told me that writing and teaching were low-paying pursuits and that I should really follow through on my earlier thoughts about law school. So off I went.

When I started law school, I was quickly swept into a culture of great expectations. The expectations were that a fulfilling career and commensurate financial rewards were in the offing once a challenging course of study was completed. Five years of focused study and articling followed. I held down a few different jobs to fund these years of study, but finances were very tight. From the first year of law school on, I noticed a very impressed response from the general public when one explained one was a law student. I vividly recall thoughts in my head that told me, "I was going to be a lawyer for heaven's sake, I should start acting (spending) like one."

And so the pursuit of the brass ring began in earnest. This was the first time that I remember hearing this term as those around me spoke of the inevitability of money and status once one became a successful lawyer. I remember my brother telling me at the time that I should have a look around me in class and start dating some classmates as they were likely to be the future leaders of the country and I could end up marrying one. My then boyfriend, who was not a law student, countered that I didn't need to marry a future leader of the country, as I would be able to be one myself if I wanted. That seemed reassuring. But once I started into the practice of law, what I found in vast supply were many unhappy lawyers. Great financial success for many amounted to $100,000 per year. For some really driven types who practised 80 hours per week, great success was $500,000 per year. This is above-average compensation, but most were living lives of great imbalance. They worked too many hours, and their health and family connection suffered for it. Trying to strive for a life of more balance generally meant that one did not make partner and was therefore relegated to a life of comparative underachievement.

I was committed to the brass ring and, of course, thanks to the confidence of my bankers, I now had financial debts to work off. I worked night and day for the first five years and was a successful litigator. I was making six figures by my second year out when I decided to found my own firm. I worked with great commitment. I mastered how to work all day and all evening by taking my Dictaphone everywhere and by working on my laptop as I sat with my husband to watch a movie. I could see that within ten years, I too could be one of the really successful lawyers making mid-six figures. But I was also feeling very much out of balance. I struggled to have time for other parts of a life while I was working so devotedly as a lawyer. As yet, we had no children. I could see that being an involved parent and a financially successful lawyer were rather mutually exclusive goals. I had stopped pretty much all other creative pursuits, and this was weighing on me.

How could the brass ring be so unrewarding? I had fully grasped on to it. People I met seemed quite impressed with my calling, my material trappings were mounting, and yet, I was growing increasingly disenchanted. All the publications and marketing geared at me as a "successful professional" seemed to encourage more spending than one could actually afford. To me, the affluent lifestyle seemed too expensive if it comes at the expense of all other parts of one's life, so I decided I needed to evolve my career further.

When I surveyed my colleagues, I found that the majority said they were unhappy with their career and felt too entrenched to choose other options. I also had several doctor friends who felt disappointed as well. It was not that they had to work hard; they were used to that. It was more the disappointment of the promise of a certain level of lifestyle that seemed increasingly difficult to afford. Earning enough to afford the things while having enough time for health and family seemed practically impossible.

I began studying financial courses while continuing to practice as a lawyer and I went back to writing. I eventually decided to leave the practice of law altogether. The typical response of those around me was generally one of great shock. Many of my colleagues understood why I would want to change jobs, but most reacted in disbelief. "How can you give up the brass ring just like that?" "You have a good brain and a bright future, how can you quit now?" "How can you give up being a big fish?" I felt like I was failing the dream, but in the end, I was more committed to the vision of a happy balanced life than I was to the practice. "There must be a better way than this," I remember telling a friend. As I left practice, I remember that there was a certain social reshuffling afoot. Was I a success or a failure? Some could not yet tell.

A few years later, I met a friend who lived through a similar story. She too had been the daughter of immigrants who had emphasized that their children pursue education. As the eldest in her family, she had risen bravely to the calling and was a brilliant medical student. Midway through graduate studies towards a Ph.D., my friend fell in love and decided she would marry and "settle" for becoming a family doctor.

This was a disappointment, but at least being a doctor was some consolation. Her husband, talented in his own right, was an engineer who worked for a construction company. The couple settled in a small town, where the wife commenced a busy practice. The couple enjoyed the status of a small-town doctor and her spouse. At social gatherings, when medical colleagues and others would ask the husband what he did, he told them he tore down buildings and they would politely nod. The wife made low six figures and her husband made less. "He is some kind of a demolition guy," people would say.

Ten years later, she and her husband had two children and she was feeling the time strain of a demanding career and a young family. Her life had little opportunity for peace or creativity. She was a successful doctor and well respected in her community, but the cost of this calling to the rest of her life was great.

Meanwhile, the demolition husband had an opportunity to purchase a company. A division was being sold off from a more successful parent company and he was first in line. The couple scraped together the funds and the husband became the new CEO of the company now under his name. About this time, the wife remembers telling a colleague that her husband had now founded his own company, and the surgeon laughed out loud in amusement. Two years later, the husband's company had really taken off. He went from earning $100,000 to earning several million dollars a year as scrap metal prices soared.

We were having dinner one day and my friend confided that she had been thinking of leaving the practice of medicine, "I feel like I am letting people down in giving up my practice, but with Mike making so much more money now, my income suddenly seems unimportant. There are so many things I can think of to do with my time now and I would like to have the opportunity for some more balance in my life, to be with my kids, and to be creative." My friend did let go of her brass ring that summer and has thrived and lived to tell the tale.

Having the courage to let go of the perceived expectations of others is a first step in being able to reach for a life of more balance, happiness, and creativity. In order to find our own path, we must have the courage to veer off the path that others seem to have marked out for us. While we are constantly looking down to see if we are on their path, we cannot look up enough to see our own. Although a professional school can send us on a linear path toward a defined occupation, it cannot in itself give us the creative solution to our own life. Only we can do this for ourselves. We can do it by thinking outside the box and mustering the courage to forge out on our own.

An inspiration to many on this topic is Robin Sharma, the international best-selling author, speaker, and life coach. In one of his blog entries, Sharma explains how he was cleaning out some old papers and came across a very negative and critical letter from someone he had asked to edit his famous work *The Monk Who Sold His Ferrari* "when it was just a manuscript and I was a very unhappy lawyer with nothing more than an outrageous goal of leaving the Law to spend my life helping other human beings get to their greatness." Happily, Robin did not allow himself to be crushed by the critic's rebuke. Although it was undoubtedly harsh at a vulnerable time, he later framed the letter and hung it up as a reminder of the commitment and courage we need to follow our own life vision.

Some time ago, I had the good fortune of attending a speech by one of the founding doctors of the Canadian chapter of Doctors Without Borders. He too had entered medical school as a young man looking for a conventional path to success. He too had dreamed of a rewarding professional career and the status and trappings it promised. What he found, however, was surprisingly unconventional. In his first year, he had a couple of very inspiring teachers who encouraged him to think outside of the box of a normal career. They suggested that he take some time to travel to other parts of the world and see the work that some of their medical colleagues were doing abroad, rather than rushing into the pursuit of material trappings and free credit-card offerings in the student lounge.

He took their advice. When many of his friends were clamouring to find the best summer internships, he went to Africa and volunteered his time with a medical group that was offering aid to famine victims. The experience changed him forever and naturally shaped the course of his career. Fifteen years later, he talks with great passion about the experiences he has had and the calling he found. Now, with the demands of a family, he too must balance work as part of a wonderful life, but he speaks with gratitude of the teachers who inspired him to walk off the beaten path and find his own way in the woods.

Over twenty years have passed since I set out to become a writer and a teacher. I am now doing both and more. Having commenced on a promised path to the brass ring, I have benefited from stepping off again and forging my own way. Every week, I speak to people who are struggling to cut the bonds of their perceived expectations from family and society. Most complain that since they are set in their path, they have financial commitments that will not allow them to veer off. This is a cop out. We must muster the courage to find our way. Material things do not make our life. Having money can be wonderful, but in and of itself, it can be remarkably unrewarding. The popular culture that encourages us to aspire to a life of things is a marketing machine and nothing more. We must see the little man pulling the strings behind that curtain if we are to have the wisdom to build our own truly rewarding life.

It isn't true that it's easier for everyone else. People must find their way through constant effort and usually by jumping without a net at least a few times. We must be prepared to downsize our list of apparent needs to a list of core needs if we are to have the freedom we need to circle back and look again. When my husband and I decided that our vision was to found our own investment counsel firm, we had dependants, many things, and some debts. We knew that if we were to have the freedom to quit our jobs and start afresh, we needed to choose a simpler life; we needed to be able to live on uncertain income for an uncertain time frame. We sold our dream home on the lake and moved to a very modest 1,000 sq. ft. bungalow. We went from two cars to one and cancelled our gardener, cleaner, and nanny. We cut our expenses by two-thirds and paid off our debts.

Many around us seemed shocked. How could we downsize so much? Didn't we miss the view? Luckily, I had already given up the conventional brass ring years before when I left the practice of law. The gift of that severance had given me the freedom to evolve again in my life path. Things can grow back if we want them, but things can also stifle our life force if we let them.

I have seen this with my own children many times. Children can offer us a wonderful microcosm of ourselves to view. When children with material plenty fixate on a thing, they often become engrossed in its acquisition. Once obtained, they quickly go on to the next thing on their list and the first item is dropped and forgotten. Television commercials and magazines usually provide the never-ending ideas of things to get.

Some time ago, we suggested a new approach to our children. Since things were largely unrewarding, what if we bought ourselves less, bought used and cheaper items, and directed the savings to acquiring necessities for others. The

Internet makes this quite easy, as there are many web sites where one can donate all levels of fixed dollar amounts to purchase school supplies, livestock, and food for people all around the world. Not surprisingly perhaps, the idea captured the imagination of our whole family. Not long after, I heard my seven-year-old explaining to someone that she would rather buy used and discounted clothes and use the savings to buy other people some ducks so that they can build stronger muscles with the protein. Spend less than we make in order to share more. Now there, I thought, is a brass ring to shoot for. It was philosopher and humanitarian Albert Schweitzer who said that the only really happy people are those who have learned how to serve others.

I am not saying there aren't any happy doctors, lawyers, and accountants out there, or that the education is not a wonderful gift. I am simply saying that practicing these professions is often not the life dream many had hoped for and if we are to find a life of balance, we may have to leave conventional paths and find our own creative solutions. I think this is a conversation we need to have more with our kids.

Psychological studies have shown that the pursuit of material wealth and the pursuit of happiness are not the same. We know that having enough resources to pay for life's basic needs is crucial to peace of mind, but beyond these needs, more and more money brings diminishing returns. Those of us who buy into the hype of consumerism in our culture report a lack of well-being and suffer from more depression and anxiety than those who aren't as concerned with money and image. It seems that having time for family, friends, health, and creative pursuits is much more meaningful to our lives.

Chapter 13
Building and Preserving a Rich Life

If money is your hope for independence, you will never have it. The only real security that a man will have in this world is a reserve of knowledge, experience, and ability.
—Henry Ford

There is more to life than increasing its speed.
—Gandhi

One of my favourite courses to teach each year is through the Junior Achievement of Canada program in elementary schools. Volunteers from the business community spend a full day teaching twelve- and thirteen-year-olds about how they can plan their life for success. At the start of the day, we begin by asking the students to pick one goal for their life that they would like to pursue. Many children state that getting rich is their life goal. I then challenge them to flesh out this idea further. We spend the day looking at what being rich means to different people and how to take concrete steps toward their goals every day.

When I was young, I remember my parents telling me a couple of things repeatedly. One was that the choices I was making each day were determining the person I would become. No choices were irrelevant and the sum total of our choices makes the person. The other thing I remember was their constant line about following through in school to earn a rewarding career so I did not need to depend on others for money. I was my own CEO and marketing department. If I wanted to stay home a day from school, I did not have to say I was sick. My mom would ask me, "Do you have all your work up to date? You know better than I whether you can afford to miss a day." In retrospect, her attitude empowered me to realize that I was in charge of my own success or failure.

When I teach the kids in my Junior Achievement classes, I realize how fortunate I was to have a mentor conditioning me with these ideas as a child. We live in a world where people are frequently lost. In setting our life goals, many of us are trying to achieve a lifestyle that exists only in advertisements. Magazines show us what success looks like, but little focus is placed on how we should think and feel about ourselves and the world around us.

I am reminded of a promotional video I recently watched for Disney Cruise Line. The film shows a boat full of laughing and fit kids, teens, and adults. Not one single overweight person is shown throughout the hundreds of actors selected for the video. Anyone who has ever taken a real cruise, or indeed gone to any pool or beach in the last few years, will have to admit the irony of this presentation. The American dream is selling the promise of joy and health, and all the while the population is quietly succumbing to the ravages of ill health and indulgence. As parents, we must demonstrate actions of self-discipline, not empty words.

I was recently teaching a grade 8 class in a depressed socio-economic area. Only one of twenty-seven students could come up with a life goal for themselves other than "getting money." Most of the young girls expressed plans to marry older rich men to get money. A few mentioned that they would then also be able to get plastic surgery to keep the rich men with them. Evidently, extreme-makeover shows and media coverage of celebrities is having an impact on the psyche of our youth. Throughout the day, we talked about the need for practical plans to make ourselves happy—plans that involve earning a living, learning things and doing things we are proud of. One boy asked if he could be a carpenter or would he have to go to university. We talked about how he could do both or either and be very successful. We made budgets for different lifestyles that each student aspired to and then selected careers that allowed the flexibility and funding levels each of them desired. Some wanted to know if I made lots of money and lived in a mansion. I told them I made more money than most people and that I lived in a comfortable house.

It is, of course, cliché to suggest that things do not make a person nor make a person happy. Getting this message to seep into our life choices can be the hardest part. Wise mentors can be in very scarce supply.

You are a far more fascinating creation than anything you could ever own, I tell the kids. You are worthy of the best imagination and care one can muster. Nurture yourself first, things will come and go. We came into this world with nothing and we will go out of this world with nothing. The choices we make on each of the days in between are what we will become.

When it comes to achieving our financial goals, there are a few concepts that are particularly useful for us to keep in mind, and these concepts are often the opposite of what the marketing machine has served us up. A recent commercial for debt counselling captured the paradox of our times perfectly. It showed a fortysomething man cutting his grass with a shiny riding lawnmower in front of a very handsome home with two new cars in the driveway. As the man smiled to his children riding brand new bikes, the caption read: "I have it all. And I am drowning in debt. HELP!" The revolution of our culture must be to cut the costly facade, sell our financed toys, pay down the debt, and walk around pushing our old lawnmowers once again. Our bodies will be grateful for the exercise. Our entire planet will benefit in our shift from wanton consumption to a model of more balance. The key concepts are as follows.

1. Memorize What Risk Looks Like

Anyone who has been investing for more than a full business cycle will note that there have been times when returns were greater than had been expected, and there have been other times when losses were extreme and painful. It is the painful experiences that we must never forget if we are to become enlightened and learn from past mistakes. Remember the securities that have been delisted, bankrupted, or now show a value of next to nil. A couple of these skeletons are useful to have in every account. Circle such positions and write, *This is what risk looks like.* Humans have faulty memories. We need to keep a record of past bad choices, lest we too easily forget.

A few years ago, there was a company called Noble China that had issued a bunch of corporate bonds at 9%. A client who held one of these bonds in her account came to me in the late '90s. The rate was about 4% higher than high-quality government bonds at that time. Although this was not a bond that we would purchase, the client wanted to continue to hold the bond because she liked the cash flow. There is a reason that some companies have to pay high rates of interest to bondholders: it's called risk.

Like individuals, companies with high debt and low equity on their balance sheet face a significant risk of insolvency.

Noble China went bankrupt and took my client's principle with it. We must remember that all securities are priced in comparison to the risk-free rate. The risk-free rate is the rate that is offered on short-term high-quality government bonds. If the risk-free rate is 4% and another bond or share is yielding 9%, the company is paying a higher yield because it presents a higher risk to your hard-earned capital. The downside is that your capital can go to zero and never be repaid to you.

Over the past forty years, Warren Buffett has earned investors in Berkshire Hathaway impressive returns—more than double the returns of the S&P 500 index. He has made himself a billionaire. He is a very modest man. He is humbled by his work. His own assessment is that "investing is simple, but not easy." Benjamin Graham stated his number one goal as a manager: "Don't lose money. Don't lose money. Don't lose money."

Taking big bold risks can sometimes work out, but remember that most of the time, big bold risks have a high probability of ending badly. "It's the plugging away that will win you the day," says an old Robert W. Service poem my grandfather used to recite. Constant humble effort, rather than random bursts of activity, will build and sustain wealth over time. We should be leery of shortcuts and get-rich-quick schemes; they have a tendency to be painful.

2. Confidence Is Healthy; Overconfidence Is a Plague

A wealthy man once told me that rich people don't need to pray anymore because they already have everything they need. An even wealthier man, who overheard this comment, said, "That guy obviously has not yet suffered great loss." The second man had lost a son in a automobile accident a few years earlier.

Lack of confidence can be a huge impediment when it prevents people from pursuing dreams, but overconfidence can be an equal detriment to sustaining lifelong success. Experiencing some success can be a plague when people fail to plan for other outcomes. Wise people know that nothing in life is permanent. Neither wealth nor good health is a static condition.

In the first chapter, I spoke of the overly confident dot-com guy who had enjoyed a big payout and then failed to see the need for managing risk thereafter. When things have only gone right, many make the mistake of thinking more of the same is inevitable. In this sense, many "hedge funds" are actually misnamed. A large percentage of hedge funds nowadays would more honestly be called "hubris funds" in their plan for magnifying perfectly expected outcomes. A true hedge is a fallback plan, a downside offset. What if things do not go perfectly and according to plan? A hedge is a good thing. What reasonable person would not want a hedge where one can be obtained? Insurance, such as critical care and disability, is a useful hedge against loss of health. Life insurance is a useful hedge against loss of life. Having insurance for the potential downside is not a sign of weakness but an opportunity to lower risk and improve peace of mind. Successful investors who have sustained and grown their wealth over many years have seen gains and losses. They appreciate the gains and they never forget the losses.

As a professional money manager, I follow market events carefully. I have many ideas and opinions about where things may be headed at a given time, and people are constantly asking me to share my thoughts. I always preface my comments by saying my opinion is just one person's opinion. I do not let my opinions or feelings decide our risk management rules.

Having the discipline to not let our hubris and overconfidence determine our course of action is key to long-term success in life and with money. Just as Galbraith warns us genius is before the fall, even those with genius intelligence levels require sober self-scrutiny to avoid or minimize epic errors. Those who think they have all the answers usually don't even know the questions.

When Ben Graham and colleagues set up the educational parameters needed to train good financial analysts, they set out the rules for study and experience to help steer human nature clear of rocky shoals. But rules are only valuable with the discipline and conviction needed to follow them. Subjective rules that can be fudged are not rules at all. During peak times, when stocks or commodities or real estate are all the rage, standard valuation rules are often wildly surpassed. Once this happens, those with a useful discipline will have to stop buying and even sell to those who are willing to pay them more than reasonable metrics support. In these times, the buyers who keep buying will switch to new rules where conventional price measures become surreal. Massaging the numbers to meet one's desired thesis is a natural course for disaster. Setting objective rules and sticking to them is key. If you do not have the discipline yourself, you need to hire the people who do.

I am reminded of my high-school science teacher, who said, "Stand for something or you will fall for anything." Having objective rules about money means you don't go over certain risk thresholds, you don't pay more than a certain range of price for an asset, and you don't invest in things just because you have money. You control your emotional responses by committing to the prescribed rules.

3. Don't Allow Others to Sell You Investments

In my first couple of years working in the securities business, I began to make some lump sum bonuses. My first impulse as an "industry insider" was to be very aggressive. The first bonus I earned I threw into my RSP and bought $11,000 of a U.S. penny stock. Within a few months, the $11,000 had become $100,000 and I was very happy with myself. But rather than collect my extraordinary profit, I let the profits run in the confidence that more were sure to follow. Within the next six months, the company shares went to zero. My $11,000 was now gone.

Undaunted, with my next bonus, I decided to buy the investments that were being recommended by our firm analysts and private client advisors. I was so confident in their expertise and information, that I opened my first margin account. Armed with a cursory understanding of the efficient frontier, I opted to buy 100% equities and lever up my risk to 150%. A year later, my losses were a smoking hole at my feet. How could this be? I was confused. The stories were so good; the Andex charts were so clear. Stocks were always a good investment, weren't they?

Finally, the penny began to drop. Good investments are found through diligence and objective appraisal. We cannot afford to let other people *sell* us investments. If we need to depend on the analysis of a person paid to *sell us* things, we should keep our money in our bank deposit. Beware of the sales industry telling us cash is a bad thing. In order for the sales industry to make money, it needs you to take your money out of your pocket and give it over.

We must undertake due diligence and hire an unbiased professional manager who has proven their ability to stick by their discipline in boom times and in bad. The person you hire should not be paid a higher management fee when they have you in stocks over bonds or cash. In doing so, you are giving even the best managers a financial reward for finding you more risk. Managers are people too and you want them to be disciplined and even-keeled in their decision-making. If equities are an excellent buy, then your manager needs to be able to buy you equities they deem worthy. If the manager does not find any exciting opportunities in equities, then you want them to be able to wait for the good opportunities to come along. Sometimes this can take a while. You need to be patient. If you are not patient, then avoid having any allocation to equities at all and just live with the prescribed rates on GICs in a passive laddering strategy. This will be much more successful for you over the course of your life than impatient impulsive decisions based on fear and greed.

Beware of those who say they are fee-based advisors and yet retain a primary allegiance to their firm's products. You should pay your advisor directly through a visible deductible management fee, but they shouldn't also collect third-party commissions from new issues or other products that they place in your accounts. The asset allocation for your accounts should be based on an independent and conservative assessment of your individual circumstances; it should not be dictated by the sales prospectus of the mutual funds you hold. In the final stage of the classic business cycle, stocks, bonds, and commodities drop together all over the world. Modern international markets are highly correlated with each other, and during these times, cash will be the only rewarding asset class. You want your portfolio manager to be free to hold cash in your accounts when the timing is right to do so.

4. Yes, You Do Have to Time Markets

The problem with conventional financial planning is that too often a static rate of return assumption is plugged into an autopilot plan. Planners aren't trained to time the market, but they are paid to get money into the funds. They leave asset management up to the expert mutual fund or wrap account portfolio managers. But the institutional time frame mentality of most managers in the ivory tower means that they do not time the markets either. Even if they wanted to, the sales prospectus constrains their asset allocation decisions so that they align with the marketing material of the funds. A cash allocation of more than 10 to 15% is usually considered scandalous or lazy. In this approach, no one is looking at the reality of short lifespans of people. The fund manager isn't concerned with the situation of Joe and Jane Unitholder having just sold their business and that their lump sum now represents the product of their life's work. The fund manager doesn't dwell on the minutiae of how significant a 20 or 50% drop in market values may be to the individual psyche and crucial financial plans. Such human issues are truly not their focus.

Like a car, a financial plan can only be as reliable as the engine under the hood. If the client is in the car and following the map, but the performance engine suddenly falls out onto the road, the car will not get to the desired destination. The client will need to look for another car or wait at the sidelines until costly repairs are completed. All the while they are losing precious time, patience, and money.

I knew we were officially into silly season for stocks in Canada when someone tried to slip me an energy stock tip in May 2006. "Take a look," he urged me. "I've already bought some." These words should set off warning bells to anyone seeking to keep their money intact. It is characteristic of every market peak, when returns have been strong long enough, the masses pile in with increasingly wild abandon. Once every sucker has been sucked in, there is no one else to buy. Beware of stock tips from people who have already bought, they are often a sign of certain death to capital.

Regardless of the sales buzz, investments must be carefully timed if they are to serve well the needs of our own limited lifespans. Buy, hold, and perspire is not a good solution during cyclical bear markets like the one that started in stocks in 2000. This means that we must have some objective predefined rules that tell us when we should buy and sell assets. Often, these rules can be fundamental, such as price to earnings ratios, dividend yield ratios, or preset profit-taking targets.

Technical and inter-market analysis offers us key tools for keeping risk in focus and highlighting when prices are relatively high and relatively low. Without clairvoyance, we must settle for actions that afford us the highest probability shot. If we buy without paying attention to relative price, we have a much higher probability of failure. Another effective strategy includes the tactical rebalancing of different assets and sectors back to predefined weights of one's overall portfolio.

If you don't want to be in charge of your own investment discipline (and few people can do this well for themselves), then seek out a fee-based money manager who has no pecuniary incentive to weight you more in one asset class or product over another. The fee they charge you must be transparent, reported annually, and no more than 1.5%. The money manager should also have a prescribed objective discipline for buying and selling investments. Train yourself to a life of patience. Good investment managers can only do the job for clients who are prepared to stick to the discipline. Too often, clients sign up for a disciplined approach and then decide to abandon it for a perceived greener pasture in a year or two. It takes at least one full business cycle of approximately four to five years in order to assess how a good manager is at executing their discipline. Studies suggest that it is easier for some people to lose 20 to 30% of their portfolio value in a market downturn (so long as they think others have lost the same amount) than it is for them to stay out of a market that is going up where their neighbours appear to be making money without them. This type of herd mentality is the arch-nemesis of long-term success as an investor.

Accomplished investors will tell you that the trick to making money is the discipline to leave certain assets before the masses do and to head to the things no one else yet wants. It takes patience and discipline to not get caught up in the madness of crowds, and unless you commit to living with self-restraint, no investment manager will be able to help you.

5. Don't Let Debt and Things Become Your Master

Creative energy and imagination make a happy life. Focusing mainly on material things can stifle it.

Many people strive to get through their daily lives just to pay off their material desires. In doing so we are often miserable, trying to convince ourselves that we are living a happy life. Living this example for our children, we find that they too may grow to focus on the things they collect rather on the things they can create.

As I write this, North Americans are into a second straight year of negative savings rates. This means that people on average have been spending considerably more than they make. To do this, they must accumulate debt to pay for their spending. This means that we are borrowing economic growth from the future to fund our present wants. In addition, many people fuel their desires by refinancing their homes and gutting out the equity they've accumulated over the years. This trend will end badly. We have record-high divorce rates and 75% of North Americans recently surveyed say that they are not highly engaged by their employment. This means that three quarters of us are getting through our days just to pay for our lives. Meanwhile, our life force and true creative potential are diminished, while our world's natural resources are pointlessly squandered.

Recent ads push credit like a narcotic to desperate consumers. We must plan our lives to spend less than we earn. If our life is too expensive, we must downsize it. If we want more than we earn, we must find ways to augment or improve our income first before we allow our material desires to lead the parade. Living a life of balance and peace means we must have the wisdom to balance our needs and wants with our abilities and resources. A little story I once heard makes this point very well:

An American businessman was at the pier of a small coastal Mexican village when a small boat with just one fisherman docked. Inside the small boat were several large yellowfin tuna. The American complimented the Mexican on the quality of his fish and asked how long it took to catch them. The Mexican replied, "Only a little while."

The American then asked why didn't he stay out longer and catch more fish? The Mexican said he had enough to support his family's immediate needs. The American then asked, "But what do you do with the rest of your time?"

The Mexican fisherman said, "I sleep late, fish a little, play with my children, take siesta with my wife, Maria, stroll into the village each evening where I sip wine and play guitar with my amigos, I have a full and busy life, senor."

The American scoffed, "I am a Harvard MBA and could help you. You should spend more time fishing and with the proceeds buy a bigger boat, with the proceeds from the bigger boat you could buy several boats, eventually you would have a fleet of fishing boats. Instead of selling your catch to a middleman you would sell directly to the processor, eventually opening your own cannery. You would control the product, processing, and distribution. You would need to leave this small coastal fishing village and move to Mexico City, then LA, and eventually NYC, where you will run your expanding enterprise."

182 — Juggling Dynamite

The Mexican fisherman asked, "But senor, how long will this all take?"

To which the American replied, "Fifteen to twenty years."

"But what then, senor?"

The American laughed and said, "That's the best part. When the time is right you would announce an IPO and sell your company stock to the public and become very rich, you would make millions."

"Millions, senor? Then what?"

The American said, "Then you would retire. Move to a small coastal fishing village where you would sleep late, fish a little, play with your kids, take siesta with your wife, stroll to the village in the evenings where you could sip wine and play your guitar with your amigos."

How many of us have been conditioned to think like the American MBA in this story? No one is suggesting that it's bad to want more than just enough to feed your family. We each have our own choice about what we aspire to and how much we "need" to be happy. But we must be careful to plan and build our life choices from a basis of what makes us truly happy and fulfilled. In this sense, our outward goals must start from a plan based within. Too often, our culture beckons us to reach for material goals based on a plan for material goals alone. Reaching for the brass ring can be a very uncomfortable way to live when acquiring the ring is the end in itself. This idea applies to everything that we do and especially our decisions about money.

When you think about it, money is basically an exchange of energy. We exchange our life energy and our planet's resources for the things we buy with money. We should scrutinize our choices and make sure that the trade of our energy—a finite resource—is worthy of the things we acquire in exchange. For example, if money is spent on trivial things—faster cars, bigger and bigger houses, more clothes, gambling, or overeating—one must consider the wisdom of the exchange.

6. *Study the Lessons of Our Mentors and Inverse Mentors*

I often ask people whether they had any valuable mentors along their path. Some have a difficult time naming anyone in particular. For some time, I too struggled to name many obvious mentors in my life. Then it occurred to me not long ago that I have had some excellent "inverse mentors." Inverse mentors are the people who make mistakes in their own life up close where we can watch and learn. In watching them learn the hard way, inverse mentors can afford us some opportunity to learn the easy way—by watching rather than living the big mistakes. When I have suggested this idea to people whom I consider successful, most can readily name some influential inverse mentors in their own lives too. These helpful souls are often found in our family, school, or workplace.

I recently attended a party, where I witnessed two different conversations that reminded me of a common human theme. One group of people was discussing a local businessman who was known to be a long-time land developer and generally a wealthy guy. The conversation was universally complimentary as various people noted that he seemed like a decent person—family oriented, friendly, and hospitable to guests at his home. What often strikes me in such discussions is how surprised we seem when wealthy people are kind and humble in their dealings with others. If the same person were middle class, would basic manners and decency attract such praise?

Another group at the same party was later discussing a famous musician who was related to one of the men at the party.

One in the group made a comment about how strange the musician is, while another said, "Well, I think anyone who is that rich and successful is bound to be a bit weird." The group nodded in agreement. There can be a genuine love/hate relationship between the haves and the have-mores in our culture. The messages can be very confusing. Aspiring to be either wealthy or nice are goals often thought mutually exclusive.

People all around us serve as our mentors and inverse-mentors. We can cherry-pick the best qualities for our own life, while refraining from doing certain things we observe that have negative consequences. It is not acceptable to be insufferable whether you are rich or poor. It is the choices and lessons we learn that sculpt our character and our legacy. Truly great people are great people every day—everywhere—regardless of their audience. Their behaviour does not change depending on whom they are dealing with.

I have heard many people over the years debating the verse from the Bible, "It is easier for a camel to go through the eye of a needle, than for a rich man to enter the kingdom of God." Many are angered by it, assuming it suggests we cannot be worthy and wealthy at the same time. I actually have always seen this in a different way. I believe that we are all capable of peace and happiness within our own minds and spirit. The challenge of material wealth is that it can prove to be a great distraction. We become smaller and more trivial when we focus more on things than on harmony and peace. In this sense, it is not that wealth prevents us from finding peace and goodness; it is that wealth can distract us from the heart of what matters with its plethora of options and choices. Perhaps where there are more choices, there can be more opportunity for making bad choices. But this is not inevitable; many wealthy people have succeeded in being forces of great good in the world.

Wise people are worthy of our admiration because wisdom is a rare commodity. Material wealth is a thing, not a person. The true nature of our character may be amplified with money, but not changed. If we are mean-spirited and small-minded, money will not help correct this.

We need to talk more openly about money with those around us. We need to talk to our kids about money. It should not be treated like a dirty secret. It is not rude to discuss numbers. Some surveys have found that parents are more comfortable discussing sex with their children than discussing issues of money. When I teach career classes to young people, one of the most popular topics is when we discuss how much various jobs and professions are likely to earn. The kids call out different job titles and we discuss breadth of income, from presidents to police officers. We also talk about the soft costs and bonuses of these jobs in terms of lifestyle and other risks and rewards. The kids eat this information up. How else does a person come to know what career would best suit their character and needs if there is no one with whom to discuss such things?

When planning our lives, we should realize that we serve to teach those around us one way or another. We are all mentors or inverse-mentors for one another. Rich or poor or in between, a life of discipline will serve both in health and wealth. More people die from overeating in the Western world than die from undereating. Materialism is more likely to torment people in their empty quest for things than it is to liberate them. Money cannot make us happy, but learning to control our impulses and aspiring to wisdom and balance in our lives can be a path to true success.

Chapter 14
Takeaways

Money has often been a cause of the delusion of multitudes.
Sober nations have all at once become desperate gamblers
and risked almost their existence upon the turn of a piece of
paper. ... Men, it has been well said, think in herds; it will
be seen that they go mad in herds, while they only recover
their senses slowly and one by one.
—Charles Mackay, *Extraordinary Popular Delusions and*
the Madness of Crowds

All things considered, successful money management is simple but not easy. The following is a list of seven key concepts that I hope you take from reading this book:

1. Market cycles change. If historical patterns of the past century persist, the year 2000 ushered in our next new paradigm for investing. There is a strong likelihood that we are now in year seven of a 20-year cyclical bear market in paper assets (stocks and bonds) and a cyclical bull market in hard assets (commodities, also known as "deep cyclicals"). This means we are likely

to see a period of much different conditions than we experienced from 1982 to 1999. We can still make money in these markets, but we cannot afford passive investment strategies that worked in the bull of the '80s and '90s. Times have changed. Our investment approach must be retuned to profit in the new climate. *The ability to exercise objective and disciplined market timing will be key to success in this current market cycle in both paper and hard assets.*

2. *Investment sales firms are product providers; they should not also be our financial advisors.* Their business model is still peddling the concepts that worked in the '80s and '90s. In this current 20-year cycle, these concepts are more likely to harm capital than benefit it.

3. Fundamental analysis of companies is a tool, but, on its own, it is a limited tool. Public shares rarely trade in line with their fundamental value for long. The market is an auction that is run by emotional participants. *Investors must equip themselves to move against mass psychology at the peak and at the bottom of each business cycle.*

4. Exchange traded funds and index units of sectors and broad markets can be an excellent way to participate in equity markets without taking on the risk of individual company management. Even so, *passive index investing is not likely to be a strategy that will work well in the "new era" of the next several years. A timing strategy to signal when to buy and sell investments is also needed.*

5. *Asset allocation should be tactical, not static.* For example, a portfolio may have an asset allocation of 40% bonds and 60% equities, but the equity weight must be allowed to float between 0% and 60% depending on where we are in a particular business cycle. When equity holdings are sold out of the market, they must be strategically placed in the risk-free assets of cash, money market, and T-bills. The risk-free class is the only liquid safe place to wait for the next strategic buys that may present themselves. Where no attractive opportunities present a strong probability of reward, wait patiently in the risk-free class. When there is nothing great to be done, nothing should be done. Wait.

6. Investors should seek their investment advice from independent investment counsel firms with the following essential characteristics:

   a. *True investment advisors describe themselves in writing as professional fiduciaries.* They do not sell their clients products. They are completely independent of third-party agendas. They are not compensated by anyone but their clients.

   b. *Impartial advisors should be paid a single flat fee based on the assets under management that is the same rate across all asset classes.* They should not be paid a higher percentage on the assets that they weight in any particular product or asset class, such as equities or bonds over cash.

   c. *Keeping management fees at the low end of the industry average will be even more important to performance over the next several years than it has been in the past.* True advisors charge a reasonable fee that is completely transparent. The client should receive a clear statement each year of the dollar value of fees paid. The percentage of fees should decrease with the level of assets you give them to manage. For example, a client with $10 million should pay a lower percentage fee than clients with $1 million.

d. *Valuable managers are able to articulate both their buy and their sell rules.* They must be free and willing to move capital into and out of assets in accordance with their management discipline.

e. *Valuable managers are not restricted to any single asset class or third-party-determined asset allocation strategy.* In other words, they should not tell you that they buy for the long term and do not pay attention to market fluctuations over 1- to 5-year periods. They should not say that they always buy stocks. The financial life cycle of real people is dependent upon the success of 1- to 5-year periods. Strategies based on infinite time periods are not conducive to the goals of finite lives.

7. *We must train ourselves to a life of patience and discipline if we are to succeed.* We must remain vigilant against our common human tendency for hubris, fear, and greed. No matter how intelligent or educated we may be in our area of expertise, we must realize that humans are constantly at risk of making rash decisions based on emotion. The more objective rules and discipline we can set up to guide us, the less likely we will be to make really big errors.

Notes

1. John Kenneth Galbraith, *A Short History of Financial Euphoria* (New York: Penguin, 1990). 16
2. Assumptions:

Desired Annual After-Tax Income (Today's $):	$1,000,000
Market Value of Investment:	$50,000,000
Adjusted Cost Base of Investment:	$50,000,000
Rate of Return:	
Interest:	4.00%
Dividends:	0.00%
Capital Gains:	2.00%
Deferred Growth:	0.00%
Average Tax Rate:	50.00%
Annual Inflation Rate:	2.50%

Starting age 40 to age 100.

I) Income earned may include interest, dividends, and/or capital gains.

II) Deferred tax liability is the amount of deferred growth withdrawn multiplied by the government-prescribed taxable portion for capital gains (50% in 2007) multiplied by the tax rate.

III) Adjusted cost base represents the initial adjusted cost base of the investment plus the after-tax income earned. (After-tax income is reinvested on an annual basis.)

3. Capgemini World Wealth Report 2006. www.us.capgemini.com/worldwealthreport06/, February 8, 2007.

4. Terry Burnham, *Mean Markets and Lizard Brains: How to Profit from the New Science of Irrationality* (New York: Wiley, 2005). 6

5. Assumptions:

Market Value of Investment:	$5,000,000
Adjusted Cost Base of Investment:	$5,000,000
Withdrawals Are Made:	Annually
Rate of Return:	
Interest:	4.00%
Dividends:	0.00%
Capital Gains:	2.00%
Deferred Growth:	0.00%
Average Tax Rate:	50.00%
Annual Inflation Rate:	2.50%
After-Tax Income Earned:	$175,000

I) Income earned may include interest, dividends, and/or capital gains.

II) Deferred tax liability is the amount of deferred growth withdrawn multiplied by the government-prescribed taxable portion for capital gains (50% in 2007) multiplied by the tax rate.

III) Adjusted cost base represents the initial adjusted cost base of the investment plus the after-tax income earned. (After-tax income is reinvested on an annual basis.)

6. "The Detriment of Portfolio Performance," Gary P. Brinson, L. Randolph Good, and Gilbert L. Beebower, *Financial Analysts Journal* (July/August, 1986).

7. www.crestmontresearch.com, January 15, 2007.

8. Peter L. Bernstein, *The Power of Gold: The History of an Obsession* (New York: Wiley, 2000). 337

9. "Interview with John Templeton," Eleanor Laise, *Smart-Money*, April 1, 2004.

10. Joseph H. Ellis, *Ahead of the Curve: A Commonsense Guide to Forecasting Business and Market Cycles* (Boston: Harvard Business School, 2005). 101

11. Mark Tier, *The Winning Investment Habits of Warren Buffet & George Soros* (New York: St. Martin's Griffin, 2006). 151

12. Maggie Mahar, *Bull! A History of the Boom, 1982–1999* (New York: HarperCollins, 2003). 361 (Peter Bernstein as quoted.)

13. Benjamin Graham, *The Intelligent Investor* (New York: HarperCollins, 1973). 568

14. Maggie Mahar, *Bull! A History of the Boom, 1982-1999* (New York: HarperCollins, 2003). 246

15. Benjamin Graham, *The Intelligent Investor* (New York: HarperCollins, 1973). 269

16. "Stars & Dogs," *Globe & Mail*. March 18, 2006. B9

17. John Kenneth Galbraith, *The Great Crash 1929* (Boston: Houghton Mifflin, 1954). xxii

18. CFA Institute, "Why Independent Research Is Still Rare" (Charlottesville, VA: May/June 2006). 7

19. Dan Reingold, *Confessions of a Wall Street Analyst* (New York: HarperCollins, 2006). 313

20. Introduction, Maggie Mahar, *Bull! A History of the Boom, 1982–1999* (New York: HarperCollins, 2003)

21. John Bogle, Statement to the U.S. Senate Government Affairs Subcommittee, Nov 3, 2003. 6

22. Dan Reingold, *Confessions of a Wall Street Analyst* (New York: HarperCollins, 2006). 313

23. Ibid., 314

24. Robert D. Edwards and John Magee, *Technical Analysis*

of Stock Trends (Chicago: Amacom, 1997).

25. "Portfolio Selection," Harry Markowitz, *The Journal of Finance*, 1952. 77

26. Starting in 1979, accounting rules required insurance companies to value the equity securities they hold at market rather than at the lower of cost or market, which was previously the requirement. In this table, Berkshire's results through 1978 have been restated to conform to the changed rules. In all other respects, the results are calculated using the numbers originally reported. The S&P 500 numbers are pre-tax whereas the Berkshire numbers are after-tax. If a corporation such as Berkshire were simply to have owned the S&P 500 and accrued the appropriate taxes, its results would have lagged the S&P 500 in years when that index showed a positive return, but would have exceeded the S&P 500 in years when the index showed a negative return. Over the years, the tax costs would have caused the aggregate lag to be substantial.

27. Peter L. Bernstein, *Against the Gods: The Remarkable Story of Risk* (New York: Wiley, 1996). 150

28. Peter L. Bernstein, *Capital Ideas: The Improbable Origins of Modern Wall Street* (New York: Wiley, 2005). 59

29. Roger Lowenstein, *The Rise and Fall of Long-Term Capital: When Genius Failed* (New York: Random, 2000). 43

30. Bill Bonner, *Empire of Debt: The Rise of an Epic Financial Crisis* (New York: Wiley, 2006). 293

31. www.crestmontresearch.com/content/market.htm "Up and Down Capture."

32. Ben Stein and Phil Demuth, *Yes, You Can Time the Market!* (New York: Wiley, 2003). 19

33. Benjamin Graham, *The Intelligent Investor* (New York: HarperCollins, 1973). 276

34. Ibid., 122

35. Fred Schwed, Jr., *Where Are All the Customers' Yachts? or A Good Hard Look at Wall Street* (New York: Wiley, 2006). 180

Bibliography:
Key Reading for Enlightened Investors

Bernstein, Peter L. (1996). *Against the Gods: The Remarkable Story of Risk*. New York: John Wiley & Sons.

Bernstein, Peter L. (2000). *The Power of Gold: The History Of An Obsession*. New York: John Wiley & Sons.

Bernstein, Peter L. (2005). *Capital Ideas: The Improbable Origins of Modern Wall Street*. New York: John Wiley & Sons.

Bonner, Bill, and Addison Wiggin. (2006). *Empire of Debt: The Rise of an Epic Financial Crisis*. New York: John Wiley & Sons.

Burnham, Terry. (2005). *Mean Markets and Lizard Brains: How to Profit from the New Science of Irrationality*. New York: John Wiley & Sons.

Easterling, Ed. (2005). *Unexpected Returns: Understanding Secular Stock Market Cycles*. Fort Bragg: Cypress House.

Ellis, Joseph, H. (2005). *Ahead of the Curve: A Commonsense Guide to Forecasting Business and Market Cycles*. Boston: Harvard Business School Press.

Galbraith, John Kenneth. (1990). *A Short History of Financial Euphoria*. New York: Penguin Books.

Galbraith, John Kenneth. (1954). *The Great Crash 1929*. Boston: Houghton Mifflin Co.

Graham, Benjamin. (1973). *The Intelligent Investor.* New York: HarperCollins

Kindleberger, Charles, P. (1978). *Manias, Panics and Crashes*. New York: John Wiley & Sons.

Lowenstein, Roger. (1995). *Buffet: The Making of an American Capitalist*. New York: Broadway Books.

Lowenstein, Roger. (2000). *When Genius Failed: The Rise and Fall of Long-Term Capital Management*. New York: Random House.

Mackay, Charles. (2002). *Extraordinary Popular Delusions and the Madness of Crowds*. New York: Metro Books.

Mahar, Maggie. (2003). *Bull! A History of the Boom, 1982-1999: What Drove the Breakneck Market—and What Every Investor Needs to Know about Financial Cycles*. New York: HarperCollins.

Maudlin, John. (2004). *Bull's Eye Investing: Targeting Real Returns in a Smoke and Mirrors Market*. New York: John Wiley & Sons.

Maudlin, John. (2006). *Just One Thing: Twelve of the World's Best Investors Reveal the One Strategy You Can't Overlook*. New York: John Wiley & Sons.

Murphy, John. (2004). *Intermarket Analysis: Profiting from Global Market Relationships*. New York: John Wiley & Sons.

Pring, Martin J. (1993). *Investment Psychology Explained: Classic Strategies to Beat the Markets*. New York: John Wiley & Sons.

Reingold, Dan. (2006). *Confessions of a Wall Street Analyst: A True Story of Inside Information and Corruption in the Stock Market*. New York: HarperCollins.

Shiller, Robert J. (2005). *Irrational Exuberance (2nd Ed.)* New York: Currency DoubleDay.

Stein, Ben, and Phil DeMuth. (2003). *Yes, You Can Time the Market!* New York: John Wiley & Sons.

Tier, Mark. (2005). *The Winning Investment Habits of Warren Buffett & George Soros*. New York: St. Martin's Press.

Key Market Newsletters and Websites

www.crestmontresearch.com
www.investorsinsight.com
ww2.dowtheoryletters.com
www.grantspub.com
www.bigpicture.typepad.com
www.pring.com
www.stockcharts.com

Index